A.A. Castor
Why Women Prefer
a Cheater

Table of Contents

Why Women Prefer a Cheater

A.A. Castor

Dedication

TO MY BELOVED FAMILY,

Your unconditional love, unwavering support, and endless encouragement have been my greatest blessings. From the earliest days of dreaming to the challenging moments of writing, you have stood by me with patience and belief. This book is as much yours as it is mine, a reflection of the values you've instilled and the faith you've shown in me. Thank you for being my rock and my inspiration.

To my dear friends,

Your friendship has illuminated my path with laughter, shared moments, and invaluable support. You've cheered me on through every triumph and lifted me up through every challenge. Your belief in my endeavors has been a source of strength and motivation. This book is a testament to the power of friendship, and I am grateful for each of you who has walked this journey by my side.

To God,

Your grace and guidance have been my constant companions. In moments of doubt, you've shown me the way; in moments of joy, you've multiplied my gratitude. This book is a testament to your faithfulness and the blessings you've bestowed upon me. May it serve as a reflection of your love and the lessons you continue to teach me.

With heartfelt gratitude and love,

A.A. Castor

For permission requests, contact A.A. Castor at:

Address: Urban Deca Home Metro Manila, 1230

Email: dev.castortony@gmail.com

Website: www.tonyc.info[1]

Printed in Philippines

---

1. http://www.tonyc.info

Why I Am Writing This Book

I'm writing this book because nobody wants to talk about it—but everyone lives it.

We've been fed the same fairy tale since childhood: that women want loyalty, honesty, and one true love. That monogamy is the highest expression of commitment. But behind closed doors, in whispers and hidden messages, in tears and tangled sheets, a different truth exists—one that makes people uncomfortable.

Why do so many women stay with cheaters? Why are some women magnetically drawn to married men? Why do women willingly take the role of the mistress, fully aware they'll never be "the only one"? And why, when the vows are spoken and the ring is on the finger, does the passion sometimes die?

These are not easy questions. They challenge everything we've been taught about female morality, love, and sexuality. But they deserve honest answers.

I'm writing this book not to shame, but to understand. To explore the parts of female desire that are rarely spoken out loud—the biological urges, the historical patterns, and the psychological truths that influence why women make the choices they do. Because it's not always about low self-esteem, lack of values, or emotional weakness. Sometimes, it's survival. Sometimes, it's strategy. Sometimes, it's pure instinct.

This book is for the woman who stayed even when she knew.

For the woman who loved a man who was never fully hers.

For the woman who enjoyed the thrill more than the commitment.

And for the woman who's ready to ask, *"What does love really mean to me?"*

I don't expect everyone to agree with what's in these pages. But I do expect some of you to see yourselves in them—and maybe, for the first time, finally understand why.

This is not a guide. It's a mirror.
Let's begin.

About the Author

A.A. Castor writes what others are too afraid to say out loud.

Blending unapologetic honesty with psychological insight, Castor dives into the raw, uncomfortable truths behind human behavior—especially when it comes to love, power, sex, and betrayal. With a style that's both confrontational and compassionate, Castor challenges societal norms and exposes the hidden motivations that drive us.

In *Why Women Prefer a Cheater*, Castor explores the unspoken side of female desire, drawing from biology, history, and psychology to answer the question most people are too ashamed to ask out loud. This is not a book of judgment—but of revelation.

When Castor writes, it's not to soothe—it's to awaken.

Chapter 1: The Biological Blueprint

How evolution and reproductive instincts shape female attraction to cheaters

Alpha Attraction: Why the Dangerous Male Always Wins

Since the dawn of human history, women have not merely sought survival—they've sought the best odds for their offspring to survive. This meant mating not with the nicest man, but with the strongest, most dominant, most resourceful man. And here's the brutal truth: the traits that make a man more likely to cheat—confidence, power, fearlessness, charisma—are often the same traits that scream "alpha male" to a woman's subconscious mind. These traits were once vital in hunting, protecting the tribe, and dominating rivals. Now, they're seen in boardrooms, on social media, or in any man who walks into a room like he owns it.

The cheater is often not sneaky because he's weak. He cheats because he can. And women know this. They can feel it. He doesn't ask for permission—he takes what he wants. Biologically, this signals not just strength, but high mate value. Not morally good—but evolutionarily successful. A man who cheats and still retains multiple partners demonstrates sexual market dominance. In the language of biology, he's a proven genetic investor—even if he's a disaster in the fidelity department.

Survival of the Fittest Genes: Women as Genetic Strategists

Here's something evolution doesn't care about: your feelings. It doesn't care about romantic ideals, wedding vows, or fairy tales. Evolution only cares about what works. And for women, what often "worked" over thousands of years was securing the best genes possible for their children.

The unfaithful, high-status male—the one with options—often has those options for a reason: physical fitness, social dominance, intelligence, confidence, or resources. Women, often without realizing it, are drawn to these markers of "better" genes, even if the man is emotionally unavailable or already taken. He represents an evolutionary jackpot. His genetic "currency" is valuable, even if his character is bankrupt.

This is why some women will risk everything—marriage, dignity, reputation—to sleep with a man who's already been chosen by another. It's not about logic. It's about legacy. The unspoken, ancient instinct whispers: *If he fathered your child, your child would survive longer. Be stronger. Be smarter. Be better.*

Disturbing? Yes. True? Even more so.

The Dual Mating Strategy: Lover and Provider

Evolutionary psychology presents one of its darkest—and most laughably honest—truths in what's called the "dual mating strategy." This theory suggests that women, particularly during ovulation, are attracted to genetically desirable men for short-term mating, while seeking reliable, supportive men for long-term investment.

Translation? She'll marry the nice guy, but sleep with the exciting one. One man for the home. One for the hormones.

This doesn't mean every woman cheats. But it does mean that biologically, women are wired to *hedge their bets*. Evolution didn't prioritize loyalty—it prioritized *options*. This dual system was a safety net in a brutal world: get protection from the stable partner, and if you're lucky, sneak in superior genes from the dangerous, unattached one.

The modern result? A woman may feel deeply loyal to her husband but still fantasize about the brooding, unavailable coworker who doesn't care she's married. She may not act on it, but the instinct is ancient, persistent, and deeply embedded in her DNA.

Mate Poaching and Pre-Selection: The Power of "Taken"

Ever wonder why women often want the man that another woman already has? It's not coincidence—it's evolutionary economics.

In biology, mate selection takes energy and risk. You're gambling with your future. So, if another woman—especially a high-value one—has already vetted and chosen a man, that's a major signal that he's worth something. This is called *pre-selection*. It means the market has already spoken. He's valuable.

This is why women will chase after the married man, flirt with the committed boyfriend, or compete with other women even if they have options of their own. It's not just attraction—it's a biological hack: *If she wants him, he must be worth wanting.*

From a darkly practical standpoint, women aren't just choosing a man—they're choosing a *winner*. And nothing signals "winner" like someone who's already been chosen. The twisted irony? The cheater becomes more attractive after he cheats. The fact that multiple women want him only increases his evolutionary value.

Hormonal Warfare: What Ovulation Does to Desire

During ovulation, women experience a surge in estrogen and a spike in testosterone—a hormonal cocktail that heightens libido and sharpens focus on dominant, masculine traits. Facial symmetry, deep voices, broad shoulders, and social dominance become more noticeable and more desirable.

And guess what kind of men usually possess those traits? Cheaters.

During this fertile window, women are biologically programmed to seek high-quality genes, even at the expense of emotional stability or relationship security. It's not a conscious betrayal—it's hormonal sabotage. The body wants what it wants, and it doesn't care about your marriage vows.

Even in modern studies, women during ovulation report stronger attraction to men who are emotionally unavailable, sexually experienced, and socially assertive—classic "player" archetypes. So while the mind may say, *"That guy is bad news,"* the body is already undoing its buttons.

Hypergamy and Sexual Status Climbing

Hypergamy—the preference for mating upward in social status—is not a modern invention. It's an ancient survival tactic. Women evolved to seek out men who could offer protection, resources, and social mobility. The higher the man's status, the better her odds—and her children's odds—of surviving and thriving.

In today's world, status doesn't mean hunting prowess. It means wealth, influence, visibility, and confidence. And often, the men with these traits have multiple sexual partners—or at the very least, the potential for them.

To many women, sleeping with a high-status, unfaithful man is better than committing to a low-status, faithful one. It's not just about love—it's about leverage. In many cases, it's a trade: exclusivity for status. And if she can't have him exclusively, she'll still take him—because being with him, even temporarily, boosts *her* status by association.

Sperm Wars and the Logic of Multiple Mates

Most people don't know this, but human sperm actually come in multiple types. Some are designed to fertilize, others are literally designed to *fight*. Yes—sperm battle other sperm inside the woman's reproductive tract. That only makes sense if women were never meant to be strictly monogamous.

Evolution expected—and prepared for—the idea that multiple males would deposit sperm in one woman's body within a short time frame. This is sexual warfare at the cellular level. And it suggests that female infidelity wasn't an accident of morality—it was a strategy of biology.

Women who attracted multiple partners may have increased the odds of conception and the odds of selecting superior genetic traits. Cheating, in this sense, wasn't weakness. It was war.

The Paradox of Female Desire: Danger as Aphrodisiac

Here's the dirty secret: Women are often turned on by risk. Not just physical danger, but emotional danger—uncertainty, unpredictability, mystery, and chaos. Cheaters are full of all of these.

A man who might not call back is more thrilling than the man who texts good morning every day. A man who's hard to get is more appealing than the one who's always available. Why? Because evolution made desire thrive in uncertainty. Predictability doesn't trigger the same reward system.

Cheaters are unpredictable. They're elusive. They come and go. They create highs and lows. This rollercoaster mimics the hormonal patterns of arousal. It's a cruel trick of the mind, but one that's biologically wired. The man who breaks your heart might also be the one who makes you feel most alive.

This is biology stripped of romance. It doesn't care about good intentions or relationship advice. It cares about survival, status, and sex. Women are not weak for falling for cheaters—they're wired by millions of years of evolution to be attracted to what those men represent.

Not all women fall. But many do. And now you know why.

Ready for the next chapter when you are.

Alpha Attraction

Women are biologically wired to seek dominant males—cheaters often display traits linked with confidence and success.

The Dangerous Male: A Walking Hormonal Trigger

Let's not sugarcoat it: women are not naturally drawn to men who follow the rules. They're drawn to the men who make them. Or break them. Or pretend rules never existed in the first place.

Biologically speaking, the male who cheats doesn't just signal disloyalty—he signals dominance. He is often confident, assertive, ambitious, physically commanding, and socially dominant. He doesn't ask for permission; he moves through the world like it's already his. And here's the part that stings for every "nice guy" out there: those same traits that make a man cheat are often the same ones that make him sexually irresistible.

From an evolutionary standpoint, this makes brutal sense. In early human societies, women who mated with the most dominant males—leaders, warriors, hunters—were more likely to produce strong offspring. These men could provide, protect, and dominate others, securing the woman's future and her child's survival. Submission wasn't weakness—it was strategy. And attraction to dominance wasn't foolish—it was survival instinct.

The alpha male wasn't just a leader. He was often a violator of norms. He did what others feared. He took what others were too timid to ask for. This man didn't "earn" loyalty—he assumed it. And in today's modern landscape, he wears a suit instead of war paint, manipulates boardrooms instead of rival tribes, and cheats in hotels instead of caves.

Why Nice Doesn't Win

Nice guys finish last not because women are cruel, but because biology doesn't reward predictability. Kindness, reliability, sensitivity—these are incredible traits for a partner or father. But for the raw, animalistic urge of sexual attraction? They rarely fire the brain's pleasure centers.

Testosterone is the hormone linked to dominance, aggression, and yes—cheating. It's also what drives a man to take risks, assert himself, and dominate rivals. High-testosterone males are often the ones who achieve high social or professional status. They're the CEOs, athletes, gang leaders, charismatic rebels—pick your poison. They're also statistically more likely to cheat.

So what does that say about women? Nothing cruel or shallow. Just this: the female brain is hardwired to recognize and respond to dominance. Whether in a prehistoric hunting ground or a modern office, dominance equals value. It signals that this man could protect, provide, and out-compete other males. And yes, sometimes destroy her peace of mind in the process.

But evolution doesn't care about your happiness. It only cares that your child survives.

The Visual Signals of Power

It's not just what the alpha says—it's how he moves, how he stands, how he looks. Dominant males exhibit a set of nonverbal cues that are universally recognized as high status: upright posture, expansive gestures, slower movements, direct eye contact, low vocal pitch, and lack of nervous fidgeting. These signals are instinctively read as signs of confidence and genetic fitness.

Cheaters often possess these visual cues. That's not an accident. They're socially confident, sexually experienced, and often skilled in manipulation—not just of women, but of social environments. These are survival traits, just used for modern conquest instead of ancient survival.

Women don't choose these men because they want drama. They choose them because the body is reacting before the mind can intervene. The alpha sets off ancient instincts long before logic can say, *"He's not good for me."*

Why the Alpha Male Rarely Asks for Permission

The cheater doesn't wait to be told he's desirable—he already believes he is. He doesn't ask if he can kiss you—he simply leans in. He doesn't wonder if he's good enough—he assumes it. This certainty, even when it's built on nothing but delusion and ego, is intoxicating.

Confidence is not just a social asset. It's a primal aphrodisiac. Why? Because it signals control. And control, in evolutionary terms, equals survival. If a man can control a room, a situation, a narrative—then surely he can protect you. Surely he can dominate other threats. Surely, he can lead.

Even when he's full of shit, that projection of confidence can override rational thought. Because the female brain, especially in moments of attraction, is not scanning for moral virtue. It's scanning for strength.

That's the disturbing truth: the very traits that make a man terrible in relationships are often the same ones that make him irresistible in bed.

The Dark Side of Desire: Women Aren't Attracted to Chaos—But to the Men Who Command It

It's not that women want pain. It's that they're drawn to the men who can *inflict* it—and often *choose not to*. There's a twisted safety in power restrained. The cheater, the alpha, the dangerous man—he could ruin her. That's what makes it exciting. He has the power to devastate, and when he doesn't, it feels like love. When he does, it feels like fate.

The tragic reality? His dominance is the drug, and the fallout is just the side effect.

From Caveman to Club Promoter: The Alpha Evolution

What once was a spear and kill is now a sports car and six-figure salary. The core traits are the same—resources, power, assertiveness, confidence—but the package has modernized. Cheaters are often these evolved alphas. They have no need to prove themselves by loyalty. Loyalty is for the weak. Commitment is for the desperate. They operate from abundance. And women feel that energy immediately.

They don't ask, "Will you like me?" They ask, "Why wouldn't you?" And women—consciously or not—respond.

This isn't just cultural. It's chemical. Attraction is not a choice. It's a cascade of neurotransmitters and hormonal responses. The alpha triggers dopamine, testosterone, and adrenaline in a way that safe, predictable men don't. It's not fair. But evolution doesn't care about fairness.

Why Cheaters Are Often the Winners

In brutal biological terms, the goal of a man is to spread his genes. The goal of a woman is to choose the best genes available. Cheaters—especially successful ones—are often the most skilled at reproduction. Not morally. But mathematically.

A man who can sleep with many women signals that he has what women want. This is why some women won't care that he's cheated. In fact, they may feel lucky he's even giving them time. "He cheats, but he chose me." That's the silent logic. It's not low self-esteem—it's high biological calculation.

And while society may judge the women who fall for these men, evolution doesn't. In fact, it often rewards them. Because sometimes, the devil is carrying exactly the genes evolution wants.

Welcome to the ugly truth. The alpha male doesn't play fair. He doesn't need to. Because deep in the subconscious wiring of human attraction, dominance still beats devotion. And until biology evolves past its own brutal design, women will keep falling for the man they know might hurt them—because their instincts are telling them he's the one who could protect them, too.

Survival of the Fittest Genes

Evolutionary theory suggests that women may subconsciously prefer men with proven fertility—even if they're already taken.

Proof of Potency: Why "Taken" Means "Tested"

Here's the disturbing biological reality: a man who already has children, who has impregnated another woman, who has demonstrated fertility in the most primal, measurable way—becomes more desirable, not less. To evolution, he's not a risk. He's a *sure thing*. And in the subconscious calculations women make—whether they know it or not—he's a genetically verified investment.

This is why women are often attracted to men who already have a family. Because fertility is not theoretical—it's *proven*. There's no guesswork. No wondering if he's virile, if he's healthy, if he can produce life. The evidence is living, breathing, walking around in school uniforms. His sperm works. And that, in the cruel logic of evolution, matters more than his marital status.

Why Evolution Doesn't Care About Monogamy

Monogamy is a cultural invention. Biology? It doesn't give a damn. It's been ruthlessly selecting for reproductive success for millions of years. And evolutionary success isn't about feelings—it's about results. A man who has already fathered children—especially with multiple women—is demonstrating what evolution prioritizes most: *effective reproduction*.

So when a woman feels drawn to a man who already has kids, it's not necessarily because she wants to play stepmom. It's because something deep in her wiring says, *This one already passed nature's test.* He's not a theory—he's a result.

And that's powerful. It's disturbing. But it's also biologically sound.

Mating With the Proven Male: The "Selective Breeder" Instinct

Let's get brutally honest. In the animal kingdom, females often mate with males who've already sired many offspring. Why? Because it's the simplest way to shortcut the selection process. Instead of taking a chance on an unknown male, the female chooses the one who's already been chosen, again and again.

This is seen in nature all the time—from gorillas to peacocks. The male with the biggest harem, the most attention, the most offspring—he's the one females fight over. Not because he's kind. Not because he's emotionally available. But because he's *proven.*

Humans are no different. Women may not be consciously thinking in terms of breeding, but the instinct lingers. That's why a man who already has a pregnant girlfriend or a loving wife can still be sexually magnetic to another woman. Her brain isn't analyzing morality—it's calculating biological success. *If he's gotten her pregnant, he can get me pregnant.* And her subconscious loves those odds.

The Paradox of the Baby Daddy Appeal

The idea that a man with kids is more attractive flies in the face of social logic. A man with child support payments, exes, and drama should be less desirable. Right? Not always. Not biologically.

When a woman sees a man with a child, especially if he's active and affectionate with that child, it lights up parts of her brain tied to empathy, protection, and even arousal. Why? Because he's demonstrating not just fertility—but *parental investment.* The ultimate evolutionary jackpot.

This is the biological equivalent of a résumé. He's not just fertile—he's a *father.* That means he has genes *and* behavior that support survival. Even if he's a cheater, even if he's in a relationship, those instincts still register as high-value traits.

It's not that she's choosing to be a homewrecker. It's that her DNA is whispering, *This one can provide. This one can protect. This one knows what to do.*

The Hunter Mentality and Genetic Magnetism

Dominant males in early human tribes were often hunters, warriors, leaders. They risked more, won more, and mated more. And they didn't wait for permission. They took. They conquered. They spread their genes far and wide.

Modern cheaters, in many cases, still carry that same energy. They're assertive, bold, charming, and often manipulative. These are traits that helped ancient men survive and reproduce. And while society now calls them "players" or "narcissists," evolution still recognizes them as *genetic alphas.*

This doesn't excuse cheating. It just explains why the same men who cause heartbreak are also the ones who rarely sleep alone.

Because in the world of biology, the ability to *win multiple women* is a signal of strength—not sin.

The Illusion of Scarcity: Why the "Unavailable" Man Becomes More Valuable

When a man is already taken, he becomes scarce. And what's scarce becomes valuable. Women may not want to admit it, but the man who is unavailable—emotionally, physically, legally—is often more desirable precisely because he's harder to get.

And if he already has children? Now he's not just rare. He's *elite.* A known reproductive commodity. He's a man who's been biologically endorsed by another woman.

This is why some women will compete for a man who's clearly toxic, clearly unfaithful, clearly taken. Because their subconscious isn't reacting to his flaws—it's reacting to the social and genetic cues that scream: *This one's already won.*

And there's a twisted form of validation in that. If she wins him, she's not just getting a man. She's getting a *certified mate.* Someone who's already been chosen. Someone who's already produced life. Someone whose genes have *made it*.

The Ego Trap: Wanting What Others Already Claimed

It's easy to dismiss all of this as biology. But ego plays a role too. Women, like men, have competitive instincts. And there's something deeply satisfying—on a primal, disturbing level—about taking what another woman already has.

It's not always about wanting the man. Sometimes it's about *proving* she can take him. That she's the better genetic investment now. That his biology, his power, his attention—can be redirected.

This may sound cruel. But remember: evolution doesn't breed kindness. It breeds competition. And in the reproductive arena, women are not always passive, patient, or polite. They're predators too.

Why the Cheater's Children Make Him More Attractive

Here's a detail most people overlook: when a woman sees a man's children—especially if they're healthy, beautiful, smart, or well-behaved—it acts as a living ad for his genetics. His sperm made that. That child exists because of him. That's not just biology—it's *marketing*.

And if those children are with multiple women? Even more proof. He's reproductively efficient. Highly selected. Possibly dangerous, yes—but definitely effective.

Some women will deny this. Others will admit it but feel ashamed. But deep down, there's often a strange admiration for the man who can create, walk away, and still attract. Because he's functioning like nature's apex male. The same way a lion sires cubs with multiple lionesses and walks the savannah unbothered.

It's not that he's safe. It's that he's *selected*. And in the twisted framework of biology, that makes him elite.

The Price of Biology: Wanting What You Know Might Hurt You

There's a heavy price for this attraction. Women know these men might leave. Might cheat. Might never commit. But the pull is stronger than fear. It's ancient. It's brutal. It's coded into the deepest parts of the brain.

The cheater is not always better. But he is often *proven*. And that proof—fertility, dominance, history—is more powerful than logic.

So the woman stays. Or goes back. Or becomes "the other woman." Not because she's broken. But because, somewhere deep in her subconscious, her instincts are saying, *Choose him. He works. He's real. He's been tested.*

Even if he's poison, she'll drink. Because he's *proven*.

This isn't about romance. This is about raw, unapologetic evolutionary strategy. And when survival is on the line, the heart doesn't get the final vote. Biology does.

Sperm Competition & Female Strategy

Studies show women may unconsciously mate with multiple partners during fertile periods to increase offspring quality.

The Hidden Reproductive Chess Game

Here's a fact so deeply buried in biological reality that most people have never even heard it—human sperm doesn't just swim toward eggs. It *fights*. Yes, inside the female reproductive system, sperm from different men can engage in actual microscopic warfare. Blockers, killers, and defenders—these are the different types of sperm produced not to fertilize, but to *destroy rival sperm*.

Now ask yourself: why would a man's body need sperm that kills *another man's sperm*—unless, somewhere deep in human history, women were mating with multiple men in the same ovulation window?

Welcome to the world of **sperm competition**—where women, either consciously or unconsciously, trigger an ancient reproductive war, and men evolve biological weapons to win it.

This chapter isn't about love. It's about biology at its most brutal. And what's most shocking? It turns out women aren't just passive in this battle—they might be the *generals* calling the shots.

The Female Body: A Battleground, Not a Sanctuary

From the outside, we're taught to believe that once a woman chooses a partner, the story ends. She mates. He wins. Game over.

But the truth is far more complicated—and darkly amusing.

The female reproductive tract is less like a tunnel and more like an obstacle course. Sperm don't just swim straight to the egg. They navigate hostile environments, dead ends, chemical barriers, and immune responses. Only the fittest survive.

And when multiple men deposit sperm within a close time frame—yes, this happens more than anyone wants to admit—those sperm compete inside her, silently and savagely, for a chance to fertilize the egg.

Women, knowingly or not, create this battlefield. And according to some evolutionary theories, they *benefit* from it. Because when sperm fight, the strongest win. Which means *the best genes win.*

Mating Multiples: A Reproductive Advantage

Let's get raw: for most of human history, the safest and smartest move a woman could make during her fertile window was to hedge her bets. One man might be strong. Another might be smart. A third might be a provider. Why choose?

By sleeping with multiple partners in a short window—especially during peak fertility—a woman increases her odds of getting not just *any* baby, but a baby with superior traits.

And this isn't guesswork. Studies have shown that women are more likely to engage in extra-pair sex (i.e., cheat) during ovulation, particularly if their primary partner is viewed as less genetically desirable. Evolution isn't playing fair. It's playing *strategic.*

She may consciously love her stable, loyal partner. But her body? Her body might be sending signals that scream, *Find someone stronger. Better. More dominant. Just for a night.*

And that's all it takes.

Why Sperm is Designed to Kill Other Sperm

Biologists studying sperm morphology have discovered something chilling: human males produce multiple *types* of sperm. Only a small percentage are the classic swimmers that aim for fertilization. The rest? They're enforcers.

Some are blockers, creating physical barriers to rival sperm. Others are "kamikaze" cells—designed to attack and destroy sperm from another man. Their entire purpose is to give *their man's genes* a better chance at victory.

You don't evolve that kind of reproductive weaponry unless you *expect* competition.

So despite every wedding vow and Hallmark card, the human body still assumes a basic truth: your partner isn't your only partner. And if you're a man, you better bring an army.

Ovulation's Dark Trick: Seeking the Best, Not the Safest

During ovulation, a woman's preferences shift. Her pupils dilate more for masculine faces. Her body leans closer to dominant men. Her voice becomes more alluring. Her gait changes. Everything about her subtly transforms to attract the strongest possible mate—even if she's in a committed relationship.

The timing isn't random—it's evolution in action. Because if she's going to "stray," her body wants it to happen when there's a real chance of conception. And not just any conception—a *high-quality* one.

This is why so many affairs happen during fertile windows. Not because women are weak or immoral. But because their biology has its own agenda. Her body doesn't care if her husband is loyal. It cares if the guy at the bar has a square jaw, a deep voice, and sperm that can win.

The Female Orgasm: A Filtering Tool, Not a Reward

Most people think orgasm is just a bonus for women. Fun, but not essential. But from a biological perspective, it's far more sinister—and strategic.

There's evidence that female orgasm may *help retain sperm* from desirable mates. The contractions that occur during climax can draw sperm toward the cervix, increasing chances of fertilization. But here's the kicker: this effect seems stronger when the man is viewed as more physically or genetically attractive.

In other words, the body says: *If he's hot, we keep the sperm.*

If he's not? *Flush it.*

That's not love. That's ruthless genetic curation.

He's the Father, But Not the Best Option

It's possible—disturbingly possible—for a woman to consciously choose a stable man as a father figure, while subconsciously seeking superior genetics from another source. This is the "genetic beta-provider split."

She may love her husband. She may want to build a life with him. But if she finds herself fantasizing about—or acting on impulses toward—dominant, physically superior men during ovulation, she's not confused. She's not broken. She's just running an ancient strategy: *Keep one man for the family, another for the genes.*

It's not polite. It's not fair. It's not even always conscious.

But it works.

Why the "Other Man" is Often Irresistible During Fertility

Cheaters—especially dominant, confident, emotionally unavailable ones—are often the men women turn to during their peak fertility window. These men don't offer security or comfort. What they offer is *biological allure.*

They're often more symmetrical, more muscular, more assertive, more dangerous. And while the woman may later feel guilt, regret, or even confusion—her body knows exactly what it was doing.

In that fertile moment, the mind takes a back seat. The uterus votes.

Strategic Infidelity: A Feature, Not a Flaw

Female infidelity is often framed as emotional weakness. But viewed through an evolutionary lens, it becomes something else entirely: a backup plan. A test. A strategy.

The woman ensures she has a provider for her offspring—but also maximizes the genetic quality of those offspring by *diversifying risk.* If her primary partner fails the genetic test, someone else gets the biological contract.

She may not plan it. But biology doesn't wait for permission.

It whispers, *Mate now. Think later.*

Evolution is Not Monogamous. It's Merciless.

The human species did not evolve through politeness. It evolved through ruthless sexual selection. The genes that made it into the next generation weren't always kind, loyal, or even moral. They were *effective*. They were *competitive*. They *won*.

And sometimes, winning meant one woman, two men, and a silent war being fought inside her body—cell against cell, instinct against intellect, strategy against tradition.

So when people ask why a woman might "slip" during her fertile window...

Why she might suddenly find herself attracted to a man she barely knows...

Why she might cheat once, then never again...

The answer is disturbingly simple:

Her body wanted better genes.

And it knew what it was doing.

This is not a romantic theory. This is reproductive warfare dressed in modern clothes. Women aren't broken for playing the game. They're survivors in a species that's still running on rules written in blood, instinct, and millions of years of strategy.

The "Dual Mating Strategy"

Women may bond with stable, loyal men while being drawn to more genetically desirable but unfaithful partners.

The Ultimate Evolutionary Hack

Let's stop pretending women only want one type of man. Evolution didn't build women to chase monogamy—it built them to *maximize survival.* And to do that, they often need *two very different men*. One to raise the child. One to help make it.

Welcome to the dark logic of the **dual mating strategy**, the most disturbingly effective reproductive tactic evolution ever produced.

This strategy says: Find a man who's dependable, loyal, emotionally available—the "nice guy," the provider, the man who will hold your hand through pregnancy and pay the bills after. Marry him. Keep him.

But when the hormones spike, when the body's craving a raw dose of testosterone during ovulation, when nature demands the strongest genes possible—find *another* man. One who's dominant. Dangerous. Maybe already taken. Maybe a known cheater. Definitely not built for monogamy, but undeniably *built to breed.*

Two men. One for the wallet. One for the womb.

The Split: Provider vs. Breeder

Women didn't evolve in a world of picket fences and prenups. They evolved in a brutal, resource-scarce landscape where children died, men wandered, and safety was a luxury. The ones who survived didn't rely on romantic ideals. They relied on *strategy*.

That meant splitting roles between two types of men:

- **The Provider**: He may not be the strongest, but he sticks around. He invests. He builds. He helps raise children that may or may not be his.

- **The Breeder**: He's hot. He's bold. He's biologically dominant. He may never stick around, but his genes could give her offspring a fighting chance in a cruel world.

Modern society sees this as betrayal. Biology sees it as efficiency.

The Woman Who Loves Her Husband—But Sleeps with the Stranger

Here's the haunting part: many women who engage in this strategy don't even realize they're doing it. Consciously, she loves her partner. He's safe. He's good. He listens. He's consistent.

But when ovulation hits, she's suddenly fantasizing about the man at work who never smiles. The guy at the gym with the sharp jawline. The ex she knows was bad for her, but whose touch still haunts her. She doesn't act on it every time. But the pull is real. Deep. Physical.

And if she *does* act on it, it may have nothing to do with love—and everything to do with evolution whispering, *This one has the genes your baby needs.*

The Loyalty Illusion: Why Faithfulness Isn't Always the Goal

Men think loyalty is about exclusivity. Women, biologically, don't always see it that way. Loyalty can mean staying. Building a life. Raising children. It doesn't always mean denying every impulse.

The dual mating strategy isn't about emotional infidelity—it's about *genetic opportunism*. A woman can be completely loyal in her heart, while her body craves genetic superiority when the stakes are high.

That's why some women can cheat, get pregnant, go back to their partners, and never feel emotionally conflicted. Because emotionally, nothing changed. But biologically? Mission accomplished.

Ovulation and the Shift in Desire

Scientific studies show that women's preferences change across their menstrual cycle. When they're not fertile, they prefer nurturing, emotionally supportive men. But during peak fertility?

They want tall. Symmetrical. Masculine. Confident. Dangerous. Unfaithful? Maybe. But dripping with genes.

This isn't random. It's *predictable.* Evolution has designed the female libido to recalibrate when it matters most: during the fertile window.

That's why a woman may genuinely not want the bad boy on most days—but when her hormones shift, he becomes irresistible. She might not even know why.

Her conscious brain thinks, *He's not even my type.*

Her body replies, *He's exactly your type—for the next 48 hours.*

It's Not Cheating. It's Insurance.

Biologically speaking, the dual mating strategy is an insurance policy. A way to ensure that if one man fails—dies, leaves, becomes infertile—another has already secured the legacy.

It's reproduction through redundancy. Redundancy through deception.

Evolution doesn't care if a man's pride is wounded. It only cares that the species continues.

So yes, some women lie. Not because they're evil. Because they're programmed to survive. And if that means getting the best of both worlds—stable love from one, superior genes from another—so be it.

Cuckoldry and the Evolutionary Price Men Pay

There's a term for this in evolutionary psychology: *cuckoldry.* It refers to the phenomenon of a man raising a child that isn't biologically his. Evolutionarily, this is the worst-case scenario for a male. He invests time, energy, and resources into another man's genes.

And yet, nature made it possible. Women can be impregnated by one man while being bonded to another. They can transfer emotional loyalty while securing genetic excellence elsewhere.

This isn't just possible. It's *common enough* that men evolved jealousy and aggression as defense mechanisms against it.

Still, the strategy works. Because the man who's being cheated on often has no idea. He's emotionally fulfilled. She seems content. The child looks enough like him to raise no alarms.

Meanwhile, biology wins.

Why Women Don't Always Choose the Best Man—Just the Best Combination

Most heartbreak comes from misunderstanding this truth: women aren't always choosing between two men. Sometimes, they're choosing *both*—for different reasons.

One satisfies the heart. The other satisfies the DNA.

This is why a woman can cry over a good man she left while chasing someone who treated her like an option. It's not insanity. It's instinct. It's not dysfunction. It's design.

Women aren't always looking for "the one." They're often looking for the *two*.

The Consequences Are Modern—But the Strategy Is Ancient

Today, the consequences of the dual mating strategy are complex: divorce, therapy, fatherless children, secret paternity tests. But the instinct behind it is ancient. Prehistoric. Ruthless.

Our biology doesn't care about your modern pain. It only cares about reproductive success. That's why some women will sabotage their own stability to sleep with a man they *know* will never stay. Their brain screams no. But their DNA is playing a long game.

The child that results may have a better shot in life. Stronger immune system. Better facial symmetry. Higher intelligence. Evolution doesn't need you to be happy—it just needs you to pass the baton.

The Ugly Genius of It All

The dual mating strategy is brutal. But it works.

It produces children who are supported by safe men, but fathered by dangerous ones.

It allows women to have love without compromising biology—and genes without sacrificing security.

It's a con game that's been running for hundreds of thousands of years.

And evolution? It's the greatest con artist of them all.

So next time someone asks why a woman would cheat on a "good man" with a reckless one, remember this:

She might not even know.

But her biology does.

And it always plays to win.

Ovulation and Risky Desire

H*ormonal changes during ovulation increase attraction to high-testosterone, often less faithful men.*

The Secret Saboteur: Her Hormones, Not Her Heart

Let's start with the ugly truth: there's a window every month—about 48 to 72 hours—when a woman becomes biologically wired to crave the exact type of man she would never want to marry. A man who is exciting, masculine, unpredictable, maybe even a little dangerous. He's usually bad for her mental health, bad for her reputation, bad for her future—and biologically *perfect* for conception.

This isn't random. This is ovulation.

And during ovulation, desire gets hijacked.

It's not that her standards drop. It's that her hormones shift the entire *criteria*.

Forget "nice." Forget "stable." Forget "good father material."

Her brain quietly whispers: *Find the one who could fight a bear, steal a car, and leave you with trust issues.*

And she listens. Whether she knows it or not.

Estrogen Rises, Logic Falls

In the days leading up to ovulation, estrogen levels soar. This increase sharpens her senses, enhances sexual motivation, and boosts confidence. But that's just the beginning. What comes next is a full-blown hormonal mutiny.

Testosterone also spikes—yes, in women too—leading to bolder behavior, riskier decisions, and sharper sexual cravings. Combined with a spike in luteinizing hormone (LH), the stage is set for peak fertility—and maximum irrational attraction.

Biologically, this hormonal cocktail isn't designed to make her think. It's designed to make her *breed.* And it doesn't care if the man who triggers her desire is emotionally unavailable or married to someone else.

In fact, it often prefers that he is.

Attraction to High-Testosterone Men: Evolution's Dirty Preference

During ovulation, women tend to prefer men with higher testosterone levels. These men usually have more masculine features: strong jawlines, deep voices, muscular builds, intense gazes, assertive presence. They walk like they own the ground and talk like consequences don't apply to them.

And here's the disturbing catch: these same men are *statistically more likely to cheat.*

They have stronger libidos, weaker impulse control, and a biological drive to spread their genes far and wide. They're not built for one woman—they're built for *many.* But that doesn't matter when ovulation strikes.

Because at that moment, the female brain isn't asking, *"Will he stay?"*

It's asking, *"Can he make strong babies?"*

What Women Want—When They're Fertile

Studies have repeatedly confirmed a terrifying pattern: women's sexual preferences change drastically during their fertile window.

When they're not ovulating, women prefer reliable, emotionally connected, cooperative men.

When they *are* ovulating, women prefer men who are dominant, competitive, even aggressive—men who are more likely to take risks, start fights, or steal other men's partners.

These are not relationship qualities. These are *mating signals*. The biological goal during ovulation is to secure the strongest genes—not the best long-term partner.

So yes, during ovulation, women may be more flirtatious. Dress more provocatively. Take more risks. Not because they're consciously trying to cheat, but because nature flipped the switch and temporarily replaced their romantic brain with a reproductive GPS.

The Cheater Effect: Why "Bad Men" Get Fertile Attention

Let's make this darker. Not only do women become more attracted to dominant men during ovulation—but they become *more attracted* to men who are *already taken*.

This isn't a bug in the system. It's a *feature*.

A man who already has a partner signals something called **preselection**—other women have already vetted him, which means he has at least some combination of charm, status, or sexual skill. During ovulation, the female brain registers this as, *He's been chosen. He must be good.* She doesn't think this consciously. She *feels* it.

Add in high testosterone and you've got a chemical jackpot: the most biologically attractive, evolutionarily desirable, and *relationship-destructive* man in the room.

And he probably knows it.

When Logic Sits Down and Lust Takes the Wheel

A woman may be fully in love with her partner. She may be planning a life with him. But during ovulation, her brain subtly shifts gears. Suddenly, the stranger at the party seems more interesting. The charismatic coworker becomes magnetic. The brooding barista who never smiles becomes a fantasy.

She may not act on it. But she feels it. And the danger is not in what she does—it's in how biology *reframes her perception*.

She's not trying to be disloyal. She's just been chemically reprogrammed to prioritize *genetic strength over emotional safety*.

Evolution isn't asking her to build a home. It's asking her to upgrade her child's DNA.

Unconscious Shifts in Behavior: The Ovulatory Glow-Up

Ovulation doesn't just change desire. It changes behavior. Women at peak fertility tend to dress more attractively, speak with more flirtation, and engage in more socially dominant behaviors—all without consciously realizing why.

They get more attention. They know they're getting more attention. And biologically, that's the point.

Some studies even show that women's *faces* become slightly more symmetrical during ovulation, their scent more attractive, and their voices higher-pitched—all to signal fertility to high-status males.

It's not seduction. It's signaling. And the men who receive it—usually the high-testosterone, emotionally risky ones—respond in kind.

The Ovulation Affair Window: When the Risk Becomes Reality

There's a term in evolutionary psychology called the "fertility infidelity spike." It refers to the tendency for women to engage in short-term mating *only* during their fertile window—often with men who are more physically and sexually attractive than their long-term partner.

These aren't random flings. These are *genetically strategic betrayals.*

She might never cheat again. She might never even *want* to cheat again. But during ovulation, when her body is in overdrive, when testosterone has taken the wheel and logic is duct-taped in the back seat, *she does it.* And then returns to the relationship like nothing happened.

Her partner never knows.

The child is born strong.

Biology wins again.

Why Women Don't Know Why They Did It

One of the most disturbing elements of ovulation-driven attraction is that it often blindsides women. They don't feel like themselves. They look back on risky behavior and think, *"Why did I do that?"* The answer is simple: they didn't do it—*their biology did.*

And now? Now they have to live with the social and emotional consequences of a system they never signed up for.

The Body Doesn't Want Safety. It Wants Survival.

Ovulation doesn't want "safe." It wants "strong."

It doesn't want the man who remembers anniversaries. It wants the one whose genetics *remembered how to win.*

It doesn't care if he lies. If he cheats. If he disappears after.

Because the child he might create? That child *might just make it.*

So the next time a woman says, *"I don't know what came over me,"*

Believe her.

Something *did* come over her.

It was millions of years of hormonal programming, demanding one thing and one thing only:

Find the best genes. Risk everything. Win anyway.

This isn't weakness.

It's not immorality.

It's the price of being human in a body that's still playing by primal rules.

And during ovulation?

All bets are off.

Mate Poaching Instinct

Women may be attracted to men already "pre-approved" by other women—triggering a subconscious competitive instinct.

The Pre-Approval Effect: Why Taken Men Get More Attention

Let's cut through the romance and jump straight into the ugly brilliance of biology: a man who is already with a woman—already *chosen*—automatically becomes more attractive to other women. Not because he's faithful. Not because he's kind. But because he's been *vetted*.

This is called **mate choice copying**, and it's not a social trend—it's an evolutionary shortcut. Why waste time evaluating a man's worth when another woman has already done the research?

In evolutionary terms, a man with a partner is a proven commodity. He's capable of attracting and keeping a mate. He's functioning. He's sexually appealing. He's got something—genes, resources, charisma, emotional magnetism—that made another woman *say yes*. And that, biologically, is the green light.

So when women chase married men, when they flirt with someone else's boyfriend, when they find themselves pulled toward a man who's already "taken," it's not always selfishness or scandal. Sometimes it's pure subconscious calculation: *He's been picked. He must be good.*

It's Not About Love. It's About Competition.

Here's where it gets darker: the attraction isn't always about the man himself. It's about the woman *he belongs to*.

The presence of another woman—especially if she's attractive or high-status—creates a competitive context. Her interest in him adds value. Suddenly, he's not just a man. He's *a prize.* And the impulse to "win" kicks in.

Biologically, this isn't malicious. It's instinctual. Women evolved in environments where high-quality men were rare. The strongest, wealthiest, most dominant males had multiple partners—and those partners often had to fight for attention, resources, or favor. In modern times, that competition doesn't disappear. It just changes costumes.

So when a woman feels drawn to a man who's already with someone, it may have less to do with his personality and more to do with this internal logic: *If she wants him, then I should want him too. If I can take him, I win.*

Why Women Often Want What They're Told They Can't Have

Scarcity increases value. This is true for gold, luxury bags, and yes—men. A single man is available. A taken man is *limited edition*. Off the market. Not supposed to be touched.

That "not supposed to" is fuel for desire.

Psychologists have long understood that women, like men, are more aroused by forbidden or socially risky sexual targets. And nothing screams *dangerously desirable* like a man who is already committed.

He's unavailable. Off-limits. Out of reach.

Which makes him—evolutionarily speaking—*perfectly suited to be pursued.*

The logic is disturbingly simple:

- If no one wants him, maybe he's worthless.
- If one woman wants him, he might be okay.
- If many women want him—and he's taken—then he's *absolutely worth stealing.*

Mate Poaching Is Not a Flaw. It's a Strategy.

The term "mate poaching" sounds aggressive. Wrong. Taboo. But in the animal kingdom—and in early human societies—it was normal.

Females often stole high-ranking mates from lower-status rivals. In primate groups, females would mate with the dominant male even if he was already bonded with others. Not because they were immoral. Because they were *smart.*

You don't waste time with unproven males. You go straight for the ones already winning.

This strategy is baked into female instincts. It's not always activated, but when it is? It's strong. And often completely unconscious.

This is why some women find themselves baffled by their own actions.

Why did she flirt with a married coworker?

Why did she feel competitive with her best friend's boyfriend?

Why did she feel more attracted *after* finding out he was taken?

Because her instincts aren't playing by the rules. They're playing to win.

Jealousy as Aphrodisiac: The Role of Rivalry

There's something disturbingly erotic about knowing another woman wants the same man. It adds urgency. Stakes. Flavor.

Even if a woman never intended to compete, the mere knowledge that another female is in the picture turns the whole thing into a game of *who gets chosen*. And once you're in the game, it's hard not to play.

This isn't about insecurity. It's about leverage.

If she can take him, it means she's *better*—hotter, more desirable, more powerful.

She may not even care about keeping him. Winning is the point.

And in that moment, the other woman isn't a victim. She's the measuring stick.

The Power Transfer: From "His Girl" to "His Upgrade"

When a woman successfully poaches a taken man, there's often a rush that has nothing to do with romance. It's about *ascension*. She didn't just win him—she replaced someone else.

She took a seat at the table that was already occupied.

She proved she could dethrone another woman.

She became the upgrade.

This is a twisted form of dominance, but it's rooted in ancient dynamics. In tribal settings, status was often gained by displacing others. Women who could secure high-value males away from rivals gained protection, resources, and reproductive advantage.

So yes, modern mate poaching may result in messy group chats, broken hearts, and chaotic family dinners—but in evolutionary terms, it's a power move.

Why Taken Men Actively Exploit This Instinct

Here's the sick part: many taken men *know* this.

They know they're more desirable when they're "off the market."

They know the ring on their finger makes them magnetic to a certain kind of woman.

And they *use* it.

They flirt just enough. Show affection to their partner in front of others just enough. Maintain mystery just enough. Why? Because they understand, even if subconsciously, that being taken is *currency*.

It creates social proof. Validates their desirability.

It's not always about love. Sometimes it's just about boosting value in the sexual marketplace.

The sad irony? The more loved a man appears, the more other women want to be the reason he leaves.

Women Don't Want Cheaters—They Want What Cheaters Represent

This isn't about women loving betrayal. It's about what the cheater *embodies*:

- He's desirable (others want him).
- He's confident (he can attract multiple partners).
- He's bold (he's not afraid to act).
- He's proven (he's already been chosen).

Even if he's dangerous emotionally, he signals value biologically.

Even if he's bad for love, he looks good for *evolution*.

And so, the chase begins—not always for the man himself, but for what having him *proves*.

When Mate Poaching Backfires

Here's the brutal punchline: most women who successfully poach a man end up discovering something horrifying.

He's not special.

He's not worth it.

And now he belongs to *them*—with all his flaws, baggage, and capacity to cheat again.

Because if he left someone for you, he might leave *you* for someone else.

But in that moment of conquest, when the hormones were high and the prize was in sight, none of that mattered. What mattered was the chase. The win. The biological thrill of *I took what wasn't supposed to be mine.*

And that? That's a high no moral code can fully erase.

Mate poaching isn't about evil. It's about instinct.

It's not about ruining lives. It's about chasing value.

It's not even always about the man. It's about the *mirror he becomes*—a reflection of how desirable a woman wants to feel.

So next time someone asks, *"Why do women go after taken men?"*

The answer is simple, ugly, and disturbingly true:

Because another woman already proved he was worth having.

And in a world of uncertainty, *that's the only proof that matters.*

Hypergamy and Status

Biologically, women tend to seek upward social mobility—cheaters often exude status and confidence.

The Raw Drive for Better: Why Women Always Look Up, Never Down

Let's strip this down to its blood-and-bone truth: women aren't biologically built to date down. They're programmed to **look up**—to chase security, strength, and status. This isn't shallowness. This is **hypergamy**: the ancient, deeply wired instinct that drives women to seek mates who are better than them in power, resources, protection, and potential.

Not equal. Better.

It's not about love—it's about survival. Hypergamy is nature's insurance policy. Because in a dangerous, uncertain world, pairing with the strongest male increased a woman's odds of protection, food, and future. And that survival instinct? It didn't vanish when we invented cell phones and espresso machines. It simply evolved into modern attraction to power, influence, wealth, and—yes—**status-loaded cheaters.**

Why Cheaters Often Win the Hypergamous Lottery

It's a painful irony: the man who's most likely to cheat is often the man most likely to get chosen. Why? Because the same traits that make a man stray—confidence, dominance, ambition, sexual energy—are the exact same traits that trigger female attraction.

These men walk like they own the world. And sometimes? They kind of do.

They don't ask for permission. They take.

They don't beg for attention. They command it.

They don't chase. They attract.

And the women—whether they're CEOs or broke baristas—*feel* it. Not because they're weak. But because biology responds to *status signals* like a drug.

That man might have three girlfriends, two baby mamas, and a God complex. Doesn't matter. To the hypergamous instinct, he's still *prime material*—because he's *already in demand.*

The Status Signal: Power is the New Pheromone

In the modern world, status doesn't smell like sweat and kill counts—it smells like confidence, money, social capital, and verified Instagram profiles. Status is the new pheromone. And the woman who walks into a room instantly scans for it.

- Who owns the room?
- Who gets the attention?
- Who doesn't care if you like him or not?

Those are the cues. That's what flips the hypergamy switch.

The man who's loud but respected. The man who's quiet but *feared.* The one other men defer to, and women orbit around. That man is magnetic—not because of who he is, but because of *what he represents*: upward mobility. An upgrade. A ticket to a better life—genetically, socially, even economically.

Cheaters often *radiate* that. They've mastered the game. They know how to show enough status to pull attraction but keep enough distance to stay in control. That's not an accident. It's a **strategy**.

Why Women Want the Man Everyone Else Wants

It's easy to judge from the outside.

"Why would she go for him? He's a player."

"Doesn't she know he'll hurt her?"

"She could do so much better."

But in the hypergamous framework, that's *exactly* why she's drawn in. He's a player—which means *he has options*. He could hurt her—which means *he holds power*. He's been wanted by others—which means *he's validated by the tribe*.

That's the brutal metric: if other women want him, he must be high status. And if she can win him, that makes her *elite* too.

Because in the mating economy, being chosen by a high-status man elevates a woman's value more than any diploma, career, or self-love mantra ever could. It's not right. It's not fair. It's just evolution, wearing a suit and lying through its teeth.

The Hypergamous Dilemma: Safe or Sexy?

Here's where things get messy.

The man who is safe—faithful, stable, sweet—often doesn't activate the hypergamous instinct. He's good, but not *better*. He's equal, maybe even less ambitious. That's security. But it's not attraction.

The cheater, on the other hand, *feels like an upgrade*. He oozes potential. He walks like he could take her places, even if he ruins her in the process. And that illusion of power? That fantasy of being *chosen* by a man who could have anyone? That's hypergamy on steroids.

So women find themselves torn—between the man they trust and the one they crave.

One offers peace.

The other offers status, chaos, and orgasmic confusion.

Guess who usually wins?

Social Climbing Through Sex: The Evolutionary Elevator

For thousands of years, a woman's best shot at changing her station in life wasn't education or politics—it was **strategic mating**. Hypergamy didn't just keep her alive—it gave her a ladder.

Marry a rich man. Sleep with the king. Bear the child of the tribe's alpha. These weren't betrayals of character. They were **survival tactics**.

And today? The instinct remains. Women still use relationships as a way to climb—consciously or not. That's why women often date "up," rarely "down." That's why status, wealth, and power are more sexually attractive than kindness or consistency. That's why the man who cheated on his last girlfriend suddenly becomes ten times more desirable.

He's not trustworthy. But he's *relevant*.

Confidence: The Currency of Hypergamy

At the core of hypergamy is not just money or status—it's **confidence**. The kind of quiet, dangerous confidence that says, *I don't need you—but I'll take you if I want.*

Cheaters often have that in spades.

They're bold. Shameless. Risk-tolerant.

They don't ask for attention. They expect it.

They don't *chase* women—they *choose* them.

And that energy? That unapologetic self-certainty? It's biological catnip.

Even if she knows better. Even if she's read the books, been through the heartbreak, done the therapy. When that kind of man looks at her like she's the only woman in the room—even for five minutes—her DNA lights up like a Christmas tree.

Because that man doesn't need anyone. And the hypergamous fantasy is: *What if he needed me?*

Why "Settling Down" Feels Like Settling

The reason so many women struggle in relationships with "good men" is simple: **hypergamy doesn't turn off just because you're married.**

Biologically, the brain keeps scanning. Is there a better option? A stronger provider? A higher-status mate? It's not greed. It's not immaturity. It's the leftover algorithm of a species that evolved under threat.

So while society says "settling down" is the goal, biology keeps asking, *Is this the best we can do?*

And when a high-status cheater appears—wealthy, confident, maybe a little dangerous—*that question gets louder*. Because even if he's a risk, he *feels* like the win her instincts were programmed to chase.

Why Hypergamy Doesn't Care About Morality

You can teach values. You can preach loyalty. You can sing love songs and hold hands. But you can't out-negotiate evolution.

Hypergamy doesn't care if he's a good man. It cares if he's a *high-value* man.

And cheaters—whether they're rappers, politicians, CEOs, or broke-but-bold bartenders—often know exactly how to project that value. They know how to walk into a room and say without words: *I'm not like the rest. I'm above the rest.*

And women? Even the ones who *know better*—sometimes they follow.

Hypergamy isn't a flaw.

It's not a glitch.

It's a **strategy** that's worked for thousands of years.

And in a world where status still buys protection, power, and privilege, women will keep chasing it—

Even if it's wearing a fake Rolex and lying through its smile.

Even if he's taken.

Even if he's trash.

Because status is still the most irresistible cologne a man can wear.

And hypergamy?

It never forgets the scent.

Chapter 2: Historical Patterns of Polygyny and Mistresses

Exploring how history has normalized or romanticized women's roles in infidelity

The Lie of Monogamy as the Norm

Before we go forward, let's break the most sacred myth in modern relationships: **monogamy is not the default setting for human beings.** It is a relatively new social invention, enforced by law, religion, and guilt. For most of human history, what was normal wasn't one man and one woman pledging eternal exclusivity—it was **one powerful man and as many women as he could afford, control, or seduce.**

Polygyny—one man with multiple wives or sexual partners—was the rule, not the exception. Kings did it. Warriors did it. Tribal leaders did it. And here's the part that society tries to erase: women *played along*. Not because they were oppressed. But because it often benefited them more to be the **mistress of a powerful man than the wife of a powerless one**.

In many cases, being "the other woman" wasn't disgraceful—it was strategic. Sometimes, it was even prestigious. And yes, history has the receipts.

Kings and Their Courts: Mistress as Power Broker

Start with royalty. The very idea of the king being sexually exclusive was laughable to most ancient societies. Kings were expected to have wives for diplomacy and mistresses for desire. These women weren't hidden—they were **celebrated**, flaunted, and often granted lands, titles, and influence.

Take Madame de Pompadour, the official mistress of King Louis XV of France. She wasn't just a sidepiece—she was a political advisor, art patron, and court powerbroker. The king's advisors listened to her. Ambassadors sought her favor. She **ran** things, not from a throne—but from a bedroom.

In these scenarios, mistresses weren't just objects of lust. They were *strategic assets*. Women accepted, even pursued, this role—not as a step down, but as a **shortcut to status** in a world where direct power was off-limits.

Religious Hypocrisy and Scriptural Justification

It gets better—or worse, depending on your level of sarcasm.

Even religious texts reflect and reinforce the norm of polygyny. The Old Testament alone lists patriarchs like Abraham, Jacob, David, and Solomon with multiple wives and concubines. King Solomon had **700 wives and 300 concubines**. That's not a harem—that's a population.

And yet, these men are treated as heroes, prophets, and holy kings. Their "infidelity" wasn't sin. It was seen as a **sign of divine favor and masculine success**.

Now ask yourself: what message did this send to women?

Answer: If you can't be the wife, be the mistress. There's power in proximity. Favor in intimacy. Survival in surrender.

The church may preach purity, but history proves women were often **empowered by infidelity**—not destroyed by it.

Marriage Was Business—Mistresses Were for Love

Historically, marriage was never about love. It was about alliances, land, bloodlines, and economics. You married for duty. You **cheated for desire**.

This is why aristocrats across Europe had open secrets about their mistresses. In fact, in many elite circles, **not** having one was seen as a weakness, a failure to embody full masculine virility.

And women? They adapted. Some became mistresses to survive. Others did it to **escape the cage of marriage** itself. Being a mistress often meant freedom from domestic drudgery, childbirth, and obedience—while still enjoying luxury, status, and the thrill of forbidden attention.

For many women, the mistress role became a **life hack**. You get the perks of the man without the burden of being his legal property.

Eastern Empires and the Harem Game

Western history isn't special. In imperial China, the Forbidden City was home to hundreds of concubines selected from the empire's most beautiful and intelligent girls. The goal wasn't just pleasure—it was **political survival**. A single night with the emperor could elevate a concubine's family from poverty to nobility.

The Ottoman Empire had its own version: the harem. Again, these weren't passive sex slaves. Many harem women became mothers of sultans—wielding **immense power** through their sons. Known as the Sultanate of Women, this period in Ottoman history was marked by women essentially **running the empire** from behind the veil.

Infidelity? No. In these systems, sexual multiplicity was **statecraft**. And women **mastered** the game.

Colonial Mistresses and Mixed-Blood Advantage

During colonial occupations—whether in Latin America, Southeast Asia, or Africa—European men often took local mistresses. Not hidden affairs, but **semi-official arrangements**, with property, inheritance, and sometimes even social legitimacy involved.

For local women, this wasn't simply moral compromise—it was **upward mobility**. Being the mistress of a European officer offered financial support, protection, and status within a colonial caste system designed to devalue them.

Again, we see the same pattern: infidelity isn't a fall from grace—it's often a **ladder out of poverty**.

The Mistress as Muse: Romanticized Rebellion

By the 19th and early 20th centuries, the role of the mistress morphed again—this time into a **romantic ideal**. Think of all the poets, painters, and composers who drew inspiration from their forbidden lovers.

The mistress wasn't just a secret. She was the **muse**—a symbol of passion, rebellion, and dangerous beauty. She existed outside the rules. She **broke the system by refusing to be owned by it**.

Society punished her in public but envied her in private.

Even modern literature and film are full of this trope: the woman who knows he's married but *feels* more alive in his arms than she ever did in her own life. Is it sad? Sure. But it's also undeniably **powerful**.

When Being "The Other Woman" Was the Only Option

Throughout history, women didn't always get to choose whether they'd be wives or mistresses. Men made the rules. Women played the game.

But here's what's terrifyingly consistent: women found a way to win—*even inside the system that was built to use them.* They turned infidelity into opportunity. They made seduction a strategy. They used their proximity to power as a tool of transformation.

And many of them came out with more influence than the wives ever had.

The Polygyny Pattern Still Lingers

Today, polygyny is less formal—but still deeply embedded. From billionaires with secret second families to celebrities who rotate mistresses like seasons, the behavior hasn't stopped. It's just **rebranded**.

Modern society pretends to punish the mistress, but still **glorifies the man who "can't be tamed."** And many women, deep down, still see value in being chosen—*even if it's not exclusive*. Because as history shows, being chosen by a powerful man—even temporarily—can still change your life.

The Mistress Archetype Is Not New—It's Eternal

The idea that women have only ever wanted monogamy is a myth sold by morality and sustained by shame.

The truth? The role of the mistress is **older than marriage**, **deeper than religion**, and **sharper than virtue**. It is a symbol of **sexual agency**, **strategic rebellion**, and **emotional escape**. It has been punished, romanticized, monetized, and weaponized.

And yet—it persists. Because under the polite surface of society, **power still attracts**, and **women still know how to find it.**

So next time someone says, *"She's just a mistress,"*
Correct them.
Say: *She's playing a role that history wrote long before she was born.*
A role that sometimes breaks hearts.
Sometimes builds empires.
And almost always tells the truth about what women really want—
Not promises. But power.

Kings and Concubines

Royal mistresses were symbols of power, not shame—women sought status, protection, and influence through them.

The Throne Beside the Throne: Why the Mistress Was Often Mightier Than the Queen

Let's kill the fantasy right now: in most kingdoms, the queen was not the love of the king's life—she was a political alliance wrapped in silk. Her purpose? To produce heirs, keep peace between empires, and remain politely obedient. She was the emblem of duty.

The *mistress*? She was the storm behind the curtain.

She was desire. She was influence. She was chaos in lace.

And most importantly—she was often the one who actually *ran the damn kingdom.*

Royal courts were not run by the best advisors or the most virtuous nobles. They were manipulated, steered, and spun like webs by women who had access to the king's ear through his *bed*. These women were not hidden away—they were elevated. Named. Celebrated. And sometimes *feared* more than the monarch himself.

The truth? **Being a royal mistress wasn't a scandal—it was a shortcut to power.** And women knew it.

Madame de Pompadour: The Blueprint of Bedroom Politics

Let's talk about Jeanne Antoinette Poisson, a.k.a. Madame de Pompadour—the official mistress of King Louis XV of France.

She wasn't a noblewoman. She wasn't born into wealth. She rose through **strategy**, charm, and sheer psychological warfare. She became not only the king's mistress, but his advisor, artistic director, and gatekeeper to power in Versailles.

She **curated state appointments**, influenced foreign policy, and decided who got close to the king. Think about that. She didn't wear a crown. She didn't hold a title. She held something more powerful: the king's attention.

And other women didn't shame her. They tried to *replace* her. Because being "the other woman" to a king wasn't immoral—it was *aspirational.*

Sex as Strategy, Not Surrender

The women who entered royal beds weren't naive. They weren't victims of lust. They were **players in the most high-stakes game imaginable**—the game of proximity to absolute power.

A concubine wasn't just sleeping with a man. She was negotiating her family's future, securing land, arranging titles, and carving out protection in a world where being a woman without leverage was a death sentence.

Sleeping with the king wasn't about love—it was about **political insurance**.

It was about climbing over the heads of powerless wives and useless nobles.

It was about whispering into the ear of the man who could burn villages or build legacies, all with a nod.

And sometimes, it was about revenge. Because many mistresses came from families who had been slighted, ignored, or crushed by the system. Now? They *were* the system.

Queens Were Bred. Mistresses Were Chosen.

Here's the cruel twist: queens were married by arrangement. Mistresses were picked by **desire**. One was a duty. The other was a choice.

And that gave mistresses immense power.

Because nothing in a man's mind is more addictive than the woman he *wants*—not the one he *has*. And kings? Kings had everything. The only thing that made them feel alive was taking what wasn't allowed, falling for what was forbidden, and trusting the woman who made their blood boil more than their advisors could make it freeze.

Mistresses had influence queens could only dream of—because **they had the king's obsession**, not just his signature on a marriage treaty.

The Harem as a Power Center, Not a Prison

Think this was just a Western problem? Think again.

In the Ottoman Empire, the harem was seen by many as a cage. But in reality? It was a **political engine room.**

Concubines weren't just waiting to be touched—they were *plotting*. The mother of the future sultan was often a former concubine who rose through the ranks, maneuvered around rival factions, and **controlled the flow of power through maternal influence**.

This wasn't seduction. This was empire-building through silk sheets and sharp minds.

One of the most powerful women in Ottoman history, Kösem Sultan, began as a concubine. She ended up running the empire through her sons and grandsons. Her rise wasn't through elections. It was through **bedroom access, bloodline manipulation, and absolute ruthlessness.**

She didn't vote. She *ruled.*

The Mistress Wasn't a Secret—She Was a Symbol

Royal mistresses were rarely kept in the shadows. They had palaces. Salaries. Armies of servants. Their portraits hung in galleries. They were **status symbols**, not secrets.

Men flaunted them like wealth. Kings paraded them like trophies. And other women watched—and learned. Because if you couldn't marry into power, you could *sleep into it.* And many women preferred that path. It was faster. More direct. And often more effective.

In a world where marriage was political but passion was dangerous, the mistress became the **intersection of both**. And that made her more terrifying than the queen ever could be.

Why Women Chose This Role—And Still Do

The idea that women were just "used" by powerful men is a convenient fiction told by people who don't want to admit that some women **used men better**.

Yes, many women were discarded. But many others **thrived**. They got land. Titles. Education. Protection. Power. Legacies.

They knew the risks. But in a world where power was locked behind male gatekeepers, being a mistress was often the **only unlocked door**. And for the right woman? It wasn't just a door. It was a *throne* in disguise.

Even today, this instinct survives. Why are women drawn to celebrities, politicians, billionaires—even when they're married? Because somewhere deep in our collective memory is this truth:

The mistress was never powerless. She was just playing a different game.

She didn't wear the crown. She bent the man who did.

So the next time someone says, *"She was just a concubine,"*

Correct them.

Say: *She was history's quiet queen. The shadow on the throne. The hand in the fire.*

And sometimes?

She wasn't just chosen by the king.

She **made** the king.

Biblical & Religious Justifications

Many ancient texts tolerated polygyny and powerful men with multiple women, shaping long-standing cultural attitudes.

Holy Hypocrisy: When God Said "One Man, Many Women"

Let's stop pretending the Bible is a manual for monogamy. It's not. It never was.

From Genesis to Kings, the most celebrated male figures in Judeo-Christian scripture didn't just take one wife. They took multiple. And not just wives—**concubines, handmaidens, slaves, virgins, and war captives**. These weren't sinful scandals—they were *sanctioned systems*. And the God of these stories? He didn't punish them for it. In most cases, He *rewarded* them.

Let that sink in: the very religious foundations of modern "family values" are built on stories of men who had **sex with dozens, sometimes hundreds of women**—and were still called righteous.

And women? They weren't just bystanders. They participated, tolerated, and in many cases, *strategically embraced* their role as mistress, second wife, or secret concubine. Why? Because in the eyes of religion, **powerful men were entitled to many women**—and smart women knew how to survive under that system.

Abraham: The Father of Faith—and Two Baby Mamas

Abraham is the founding patriarch of Judaism, Christianity, and Islam. The original man of God. The man with whom God made a covenant. A symbol of obedience, faith, and spiritual greatness.

He also **slept with his servant girl because his wife told him to.**

That's not a rumor. That's *Genesis 16.* His wife, Sarah, was barren and desperate for a child. So what did she do? She handed over her slave, Hagar, and told Abraham to impregnate her. Not only did he do it—he *didn't even hesitate.*

No thunderbolt from heaven. No divine rebuke. In fact, God later blessed both sons—Isaac from Sarah, and Ishmael from Hagar. So what does this teach the faithful?

That a righteous man can have multiple women, father children by both, and still be considered the chosen one. Monogamy? Optional. Holiness? Still intact.

Jacob: Four Women, Twelve Sons, and Zero Guilt

Jacob, another major patriarch, had two wives—Leah and Rachel—and two concubines—Bilhah and Zilpah. With these four women, he fathered the **twelve tribes of Israel.**

Let's repeat that: **the foundation of the entire nation of Israel is built on a man with four simultaneous sexual partners.** And yet Jacob is revered. His name was changed by God to *Israel.* He is considered a prophet. A man of God.

No one asks how Leah felt about Rachel. Or how Bilhah felt about being passed around. Because the story doesn't care. **Their emotions weren't holy—his legacy was.**

And from a woman's point of view? If you couldn't be the chosen wife, being the baby mama of a tribe wasn't a bad deal.

David: The Man After God's Own Heart—and a Bedroom Full of Sin

King David is one of the most complex and glorified figures in biblical history. He killed giants, wrote psalms, ruled with power—and **kept an entire harem.**

He had multiple wives, countless concubines, and still went after Bathsheba, a married woman. He saw her bathing from the roof, desired her, slept with her, got her pregnant, then **had her husband killed to cover it up.**

And yet? God punished him *mildly*. His child with Bathsheba died, sure. But then God let him marry her anyway. They had Solomon together. You know, the wisest man who ever lived. No permanent disgrace. No eternal damnation.

David remained the blueprint of masculinity in scripture. Not despite his sexual conquests. **Partly because of them.**

Solomon: The Holy Harem King

Solomon didn't even pretend to hide it. He had **700 wives and 300 concubines.** Let that number sink in. A thousand women. And he wasn't seen as corrupt. He was seen as *blessed*.

God gave Solomon supernatural wisdom, immense wealth, and divine favor—even as he filled his palace with women from every surrounding kingdom. The Bible does eventually critique Solomon for letting his wives influence his religious practices—but it never condemns the number of women he slept with.

That wasn't the sin. That was the *perk of power*.

And for those women? Being in Solomon's court—even as a concubine—was safer, wealthier, and more prestigious than being the wife of a local shepherd. It was a political upgrade, a survival move, and for some, a **path to influence**.

The New Testament Doesn't Fix This—It Ignores It

By the time Jesus arrives, things shift. Monogamy becomes a moral talking point. But even then, the New Testament never clearly bans polygyny. Paul recommends that deacons and elders have "one wife"—which implies that **others may have more.**

The early Christian church tolerated polygyny for centuries. Even now, in some branches of Christianity, it still does. Especially in Africa and certain Orthodox traditions.

Why? Because religious morality isn't always based on divine truth. It's based on **what power needs to stay in power**. And historically, **powerful men have always wanted more than one woman.** So religion adapted. And women adjusted.

Islam and the Four-Wife Rule

Islam is more explicit: men may marry up to four wives *if* they can treat them all equally. It's written in the Qur'an. It's not considered lustful—it's considered lawful. And many of the Prophet Muhammad's companions had multiple wives.

Even the Prophet himself had up to eleven wives and concubines. These women weren't hidden. They were **honored**, educated, and politically involved.

Polygyny in Islam was not shameful. It was considered **a right of men and a mercy to women**—especially widows, captives, and socially vulnerable females who would otherwise be left destitute.

Was it romantic? No. But it was real. And for many women, **sharing a man was better than having no man at all.**

Religious Polygyny = Institutionalized Hypergamy

All of this—across Christianity, Judaism, Islam—reinforces one brutal truth: **religion codified women's hypergamous instincts into divine law.**

Women sought men with power, resources, and divine favor. Men who could protect, provide, and elevate them. And religion said, "That's fine—just make sure he sacrifices a goat and says his prayers."

Mistresses, concubines, secondary wives—they weren't rebels. They were **sanctioned survivalists.** Their arrangement wasn't scandalous. It was spiritual. God didn't curse them. God absorbed them into the system.

And that system still echoes in the modern world.

Modern Morality, Ancient Scripts

Today, people clutch their pearls at mistresses, side chicks, and secret families. But those same people worship biblical figures who had harems. They quote scripture written by men who would've laughed at the idea of one-woman commitment.

They think loyalty is godly. But their gods never demanded it.

So when a woman today chooses to be "the other woman," when she finds herself in the arms of a married man with power, status, or wealth—maybe she's not morally lost. Maybe she's just following the oldest script in the world:

If God didn't punish the kings, why should I punish myself?

Religion didn't kill polygyny.

It **justified it. Glorified it. Built kingdoms on it.**

And women?

They adapted. They survived.

And in many cases—**they won.**

Victorian Affairs and the "Madonna-Whore" Dichotomy

The repression of female sexuality led women to rebel in hidden affairs, often preferring passionate men.

Two Women in One Body: The Sick Split Society Demanded

The Victorian era didn't just repress female sexuality—it surgically split it into two conflicting identities. Women were either the **Madonna**: pure, passive, saintly, and suitable for marriage—or the **Whore**: passionate, sexual, corrupted, and disposable. There was no in-between. There was no spectrum. Just two boxes. Two cages.

The Madonna got the ring. The Whore got the orgasms.

The wife got the household. The mistress got the hunger.

One was honored publicly, the other was devoured in secret.

And here's the punchline: many women **played both roles**—not because they were confused, but because society left them no other choice. They became saints by day and sinners by night, burying their true desires beneath corsets, corsages, and coded letters to lovers they weren't allowed to want.

The Victorian woman wasn't sexually cold. She was sexually *trapped*—and many of them, in secret rebellion, **lit the cage on fire**.

Marriage as Morality, Not Desire

In the 19th century, a woman's value was measured by how well she could **deny herself**. She wasn't praised for sexual curiosity—she was applauded for not having any. Virginity wasn't just prized; it was fetishized. A woman who expressed desire was labeled unnatural, unladylike, or insane.

And marriage? It wasn't a celebration of love. It was a **contract of control**. A wife was expected to be docile, faithful, and sexually available only for reproduction. Her body wasn't her own—it belonged to her husband and the morality police known as "society."

So what happened to the women who craved more than duty?

They rebelled. Quietly. Boldly. With their hearts and their hips.

The Affair as Escape: Why Forbidden Love Was Better

For many Victorian women, affairs weren't about betrayal—they were about *breathing*. The men they married were often cold, controlling, or emotionally distant. The men they desired? Poets. Painters. Revolutionaries. Scandalous creatures who drank, sinned, and actually *looked at them* like they were more than breeding stock.

In public, these women wore pearls and silence.

In private, they chased passion with shaking hands and urgent letters.

They met lovers in gardens, in carriages, in candlelit parlors. They carved out slivers of freedom between tea times and social obligations. Because in a world where female pleasure was demonized, every orgasm was an act of revolution.

The Rise of the Gentleman Lover

The Victorian era may have caged women, but it also birthed a very specific male archetype: the **gentleman lover**. This man was not the stoic husband or the moral preacher. He was well-read, well-dressed, and *dangerous in all the right ways*.

He wasn't just an escape. He was a fantasy. He represented everything her husband wasn't allowed to be: attentive, passionate, hungry. And he knew the rules—**seduce, don't demand. Listen, don't command.** He understood that women weren't cold—they were starved.

He was the antidote to the Madonna-Wife. And many women *chose him*, even if it cost them their reputation, their social standing, or their peace.

Freud, Hysteria, and the Weaponization of Female Desire

Sigmund Freud made his name in the Victorian period by diagnosing women with "hysteria," a catch-all diagnosis for basically any woman who felt too much, wanted too much, or acted outside her domestic role.

Symptoms of hysteria? Sexual frustration, mood swings, emotional outbursts—aka, *being a human being in a corset.*

Treatment? Medicalized orgasms via early vibrators, or being institutionalized.

Let's pause here.

Women were literally locked in asylums for wanting sex.

Or worse—*diagnosed, treated, and returned to husbands who had no idea what to do with a living, breathing, sensual wife.*

This is the world Victorian women lived in. A world that told them desire was illness. Passion was poison. And rebellion was madness.

Is it any wonder they chose affairs? Affairs weren't moral failures. They were **mental survival.**

Literature as a Safe Confession Booth

Because they couldn't say it aloud, many Victorian women poured their truth into novels. Works like *Madame Bovary*, *Anna Karenina*, and *The Awakening* explored women stepping outside the role of wife and diving into the dangerous waters of forbidden love.

They weren't heroes. They weren't always victims. But they were **honest.**

These stories weren't just fiction—they were warnings, whispers, and sometimes, guides. They told women:

You are not alone. You are not broken. You are just living in a system that punishes you for being alive in your own body.

And many women read those books in secret, holding them like mirrors, seeing their own rebellion reflected on every page.

The Whore Got the Passion, But the Madonna Got the Praise

The tragedy of the Madonna-Whore dichotomy is that women could never win. If they suppressed their sexuality, they were frigid. If they embraced it, they were sluts. There was no middle. No sanctuary.

So women split themselves in two.

They played the Madonna for society—and the Whore in whispers.

One woman cooked the meals. The other sent the love letters.

One woman birthed the child. The other risked everything for a kiss.

The affair wasn't a weakness. It was a declaration: *I will not die in your purity prison.*

The Legacy Lingers

Don't think this is ancient history. The Madonna-Whore complex is alive today—on Instagram, in marriages, in church pews and pop culture. Women are still punished for being sexual. Still called too much, too wild, too free. And many still hide their truth under layers of polite femininity.

But the instinct to rebel? Still there.

The fire to be seen, touched, *wanted*? Still burning.

And when the right man appears—charming, confident, just dangerous enough to make her heart race and her hands shake—some women still leap. Not because they're bad wives. But because *they were never allowed to be whole women.*

The Victorian affair wasn't just about sex.

It was about reclaiming a body, a soul, a desire that the world said didn't belong to her.

She didn't betray her marriage.

She betrayed the **lie** that said she wasn't supposed to want more.

And sometimes? That was the only honest thing she ever did.

Colonial Mistress Culture

Across empires, local mistresses of foreign conquerors were sometimes empowered, not shamed.

When the Empire Came, So Did the Men—And So Did the Arrangements

Colonialism wasn't just about land, gold, and religion. It was about **men arriving where they didn't belong, claiming everything—including women.** But what often gets ignored in history class is what happened *after* the soldiers unloaded their ships and the missionaries finished their sermons: **the rise of the colonial mistress**—the native woman who slept with, lived with, and sometimes bore children for the foreign men who ruled her country.

And here's the twist: while many might imagine these women as victims of exploitation—and yes, many were—others weren't just surviving. They were **thriving**. Protected, elevated, and in some cases, more powerful than the local elites who judged them from behind church walls.

This wasn't love. This was **strategy**. A game of proximity to power played with the body, the mind, and the full awareness that in a colonized world, **sex could be currency**—and mistresses knew how to spend it.

From Conquest to Consort: The Power in the Bedroom

Across Africa, Southeast Asia, the Caribbean, and Latin America, colonial men rarely came with wives. They came with ambition, arrogance, and libido. And in the absence of European women, local women became more than companions—they became **liaisons, interpreters, cultural guides, and political leverage**.

These weren't just one-night stands. They were arrangements—some formal, some informal—between white colonizers and native women. In many places, it was openly accepted. In others, it was quietly tolerated. But everywhere, it reshaped the social order.

Being a mistress wasn't a mark of shame—it was a **pathway to protection**.

From the slums to the compound, women who aligned themselves with colonial officials found access to money, status, and relative safety. In a world built on exploitation, this was one of the few ways to **flip the script**—or at least *negotiate the terms*.

The Mestiza Advantage: Mixed Blood, Mixed Power

One of the most visible outcomes of colonial mistress culture was the rise of the **mixed-race elite**—children born of local mothers and European fathers. These children were often given better education, better jobs, and better legal protections than their fully native peers.

And the mothers? They became **matriarchs of a new class**, wielding soft power through their children and direct influence over their European lovers. In places like the Philippines, the mestiza became a symbol of beauty and aspiration—not a cautionary tale. She was *admired*, *envied*, and *imitated*. She didn't marry a colonizer—she *captivated* one.

Even in societies that claimed to value purity, these women found ways to **leverage impurity into influence**. They used what they had, because no one was handing them anything else.

The French Indochina Model: "A Wife Until We Leave"

In French colonies like Vietnam and Cambodia, a practice known as **"concubinage"** became widespread. French men took local mistresses openly—often providing them with homes, stipends, and unofficial wifely status. These arrangements were not just accepted—they were institutionalized.

The woman was referred to as "femme," and everyone understood: *She was his until he left.* The unspoken expiration date didn't make her powerless—it made her **urgent, tactical, and sometimes revered.**

Many of these women used the relationship to lift their families out of poverty, secure their children's futures, and establish social clout. The French man got affection, loyalty, and sex. The local woman got **access to the ruling class.** Mutual exploitation? Perhaps. But in the twisted rules of colonialism, it was often the *only way a native woman could play the game.*

British Shame, Private Gain

The British were more discreet—and more hypocritical. In colonies like India, Burma, and Nigeria, British officers and civil servants frequently engaged in sexual relationships with local women, even fathering children. But unlike the French, they cloaked these relationships in **denial and silence.**

Still, everyone knew. The servants knew. The officers' peers knew. Sometimes, even the British wives back home knew.

And the women? They endured whispers and judgment, yes. But they also received **homes, money, protection, and status** that their fellow countrywomen did not. They couldn't vote. They couldn't own land. But they could *influence* the most powerful men in the colony—sometimes with a smile, sometimes with a child, sometimes with a threat.

Colonial Shame Was a Local Weapon—Not a Global One

Let's be clear: the mistress was often judged *more* harshly by her own people than by the colonizers. European men rarely cared what the local village or barrio thought. But for the woman, returning to her own community meant **wearing a scarlet letter.**

And yet—many didn't care. Because the benefits outweighed the shame. The whispers didn't feed their families. But the European officer's money *did.* The stares didn't secure safety during political unrest. But the colonizer's affection *might.*

So they made the trade. Not blindly. Not out of lust or naivety. But out of **calculation.**

The Mistress as Political Pawn and Player

Some mistresses went beyond domestic roles and entered the realm of politics. In colonized courts, the local mistress could become the kingmaker—the one who whispered in the ears of governors and generals.

She passed messages. She facilitated bribes. She negotiated deals. She played one power against another. And sometimes, she changed the course of history.

She wasn't on the payroll—but she was in the room.

She wasn't on the flag—but she was in the plan.

And when she spoke, powerful men listened—even if they never admitted it.

Was It Love? Sometimes. But That Wasn't the Point.

Some colonial relationships were genuine. Some were romantic. Some even ended in marriage or lifelong partnership. But most were transactional. And that doesn't make them any less **real**. It just makes them **honest**.

Women knew what they were getting into. So did the men. But only the women carried the social cost. The man returned home a hero. The woman was often left behind with children, silence, and a reputation.

Still—many would do it again. Because for a woman in a colonized world, being a mistress wasn't just survival. It was **strategy**.

The Legacy of Colonial Mistress Culture Still Echoes

Look around post-colonial societies today, and you'll see the shadows of this culture. The mixed-race elites. The neighborhoods where lighter skin still signals beauty. The obsession with foreign accents. The women who still seek power not in parliament—but in a rich man's gaze.

Call it internalized colonization. Call it survival instinct passed through generations. Either way, the legacy lives.

Because while the empires may have left, the old rules haven't fully died. And women still remember what their ancestors learned the hard way:

If you can't own the empire,
own the man who runs it.

So no, the colonial mistress was not just a victim.

She was not just a statistic.

She was not just the other woman.

She was the **mirror of power, the weapon of femininity, and the survivor of a system that tried to bury her under shame—**

but only made her more dangerous.

Marriage as a Transaction, Love as Rebellion

H*istorically, marriages were economic, not romantic—emotional and sexual satisfaction often came from affairs.*

Forget the Fairytale: Marriage Was a Deal, Not a Dream

If you still believe marriage was ever about love, congratulations—you've swallowed centuries of propaganda. For most of human history, marriage wasn't about butterflies. It was about **bargains.**

Two families merged assets. Political alliances were sealed. Dowries were exchanged. Land was secured. Bloodlines were protected. Property was passed through wombs. That's what marriage was—a **business arrangement wrapped in holy language**.

Love? Love was irrelevant.

Desire? Suspicious.

Passion? Dangerous.

Those belonged outside the marriage—hidden, whispered, or punished. Because marriage was **about duty, not ecstasy**. And when women dared to want more than that, they didn't write letters to the priest. They wrote love notes to someone else's husband.

The Wife Was the Deal. The Lover Was the Escape.

Wives weren't chosen for love. They were selected like livestock—based on status, connections, fertility, and obedience. Her role was to secure the home, bear heirs, and stay respectable. She was the *anchor*.

But anchors don't fly. Anchors don't thrill. Anchors don't set your soul on fire.

So where did men go when they wanted pleasure? The **mistress.** The courtesan. The actress. The neighbor's wife. And where did women go when they wanted passion? **Anywhere but home**.

Affairs weren't a betrayal of the marriage. They were an **unspoken extension of it**—the part where people actually felt something.

The Church Said "Til Death Do Us Part." Reality Said "Until I Meet Someone Else."

Organized religion framed marriage as sacred. Indissoluble. But even inside these "divine" unions, **infidelity was baked into the structure**.

Kings had queens and dozens of mistresses. Nobles had arranged marriages and secret lovers. Even clergymen, who preached chastity, often had women on the side—sometimes entire households of them.

Everyone knew. No one said it out loud. Because the real function of marriage was **not moral purity—it was societal stability**.

It didn't matter who you slept with as long as you **passed your land to legitimate sons**, kept up appearances, and followed the rituals.

Women knew this too. They may not have had legal rights or economic independence, but they understood the system. And when love came knocking—unexpected, dangerous, real—they opened the door. Because it was the **only part of their lives they actually chose.**

Affairs Were Not Sin. They Were Freedom.

When a woman in the 18th or 19th century had an affair, she wasn't just looking for sex. She was reaching for **something forbidden but profoundly human**: emotional recognition.

Affairs gave women something marriage rarely did—**intimacy without control**. The thrill of being seen, touched, desired not as a mother, wife, or vessel, but as a *woman*.

She wasn't escaping her husband. She was escaping her **role**. Her status as a domestic tool. Her identity as "belonging to someone."

An affair was her way of saying: *I belong to myself—even if only for an hour.*

Men Cheated for Access. Women Cheated for Aliveness.

Let's get painfully specific. Historically, men cheated because they could. The power imbalance was so massive that a man's affairs were often *expected*—even celebrated.

For women, the risk was higher. Affairs could mean ruin. Scandal. Exile. Death.

So when women cheated, they did it **knowing full well what they stood to lose.** That's what made it revolutionary.

It wasn't just lust—it was *defiance.* A woman who took a lover claimed something that society told her didn't belong to her: **her body, her pleasure, her choice.**

She wasn't chasing orgasms. She was chasing **herself**—before marriage erased her entirely.

Dowries and Deals: The Cold Math of Matrimony

Let's talk numbers. Marriage in many cultures was a literal transaction. The groom paid a bride price. The bride brought a dowry. Fathers negotiated terms like landowners brokering livestock trades. Daughters were investments, not individuals.

The better the dowry, the better the husband. Love had nothing to do with it.

And once she was married, a woman was often legally absorbed by her husband. Her property? His. Her body? His. Her children? His. Her future? Tied to his whims, his income, and his approval.

So yes, when a woman found a man who treated her like a person, not a possession, she took the risk. Because even a fleeting connection with someone who **saw her** was worth more than a lifetime spent being **owned**.

Passion Wasn't Allowed, So It Was Worshipped in Secret

Read the letters. The journals. The poems.

The way women wrote about their lovers was not casual. It was **sacred**. These men weren't just distractions—they were *mirrors* of the selves these women weren't allowed to become.

To be desired outside of marriage was to be **real** again. Not as a domestic machine. Not as a legal obligation. But as *flesh and fire and madness*. Women risked everything for that. And many did it with full awareness of the consequences.

Because sometimes, **shame was better than numbness.**

The Real Adultery Was the System, Not the Affair

Let's get brutally honest: the real betrayal wasn't in the secret letters, the back-room rendezvous, or the midnight confessions.

The real betrayal was society's insistence that a woman should find fulfillment in a structure built to contain her, not nourish her.

It told her:

- "Marry him for status."
- "Stay with him for the children."
- "Don't ask for more."
- "You're lucky to be chosen at all."

And when she asked, "What about love?"

It said, *"That's not your job."*

So she found love elsewhere. Not always safely. Not always wisely. But always *bravely*.

Affairs Were the Only Honest Emotion in a Dishonest Structure

Marriages were contracts. But affairs? Affairs were **confessions**.

They said what could not be said.

They fulfilled what was never supposed to be fulfilled.

They exposed the lie that duty was enough.

And every time a woman took a lover, she didn't just break her vows—**she broke the illusion that she was satisfied being less than alive.**

So no, love didn't ruin marriages.

Love **exposed** them.

And sometimes?

Cheating wasn't the sin.

Staying silent was.

Wartime Love and Cheating

Absence during wars often normalized infidelity, especially when survival and support were at stake.

When Love Went to War, Morality Stayed Behind

War doesn't just break nations. It breaks norms. And nowhere is that more disturbingly clear than in the quiet bedrooms and bombed-out towns where **fidelity quietly died** the moment the soldiers marched away.

We like to think of wartime women as patient. As loyal. As noble statues waiting at the window. But the truth is messier, darker, and far more human: **when men went to war, many women found comfort, companionship, protection—and yes, sex—somewhere else**.

This wasn't always about passion. It wasn't always about betrayal. Sometimes, it was about **survival**. Other times? It was about **revenge**. But often, it was about something far more primal and honest: *being touched before the world ends.*

The Husband at War. The Lover at Home.

World War I. World War II. The Vietnam War. Countless others before and after. What they all have in common? **Mass separation**. Millions of men vanished from their homes, sometimes for years, with no promise of return.

Women were left behind to raise children, manage farms, fix machines, and navigate a society in collapse. And in those cracks—where fear lived and loneliness screamed—**love, lust, and temporary salvation slipped in**.

It started with the neighbor helping with the fence.

The soldier too injured to return to the front.

The officer stationed nearby.

The widow next door.

No rings exchanged. No letters written. Just **flesh and need and the unspoken permission of crisis.**

When Survival Meant Lying on Your Back

Let's talk reality. In occupied territories during World War II, local women often slept with enemy soldiers—not because they were traitors, but because it was **the only way to survive.**

In Nazi-occupied France, many women had affairs with German officers. They were fed, clothed, protected from violence. And when the war ended, they were publicly humiliated—heads shaved, paraded through streets. Branded as collaborators.

But what no one wanted to admit was that **those same people who threw stones at them ate food bought with German rations**. The hypocrisy was grotesque. These women weren't just shamed for sleeping with the enemy. They were shamed for *surviving the war the only way they could.*

Because when your children are starving, and a soldier offers a loaf of bread in exchange for a night—you say yes. And you cry after. But your baby eats.

Infidelity as Insurance

Even in non-occupied countries, wartime infidelity flourished. It was often unspoken but widely understood: *he's gone, she's alone, anything could happen.*

And for good reason. Letters were slow. Death was fast. A man could vanish in the trenches or be vaporized by a bomb, and you'd only find out months later. The emotional logic was cruel but sound: **why stay loyal to a ghost?**

So women hedged their emotional bets. Some found comfort. Others found passion. Some just wanted to feel something before the next bomb dropped. And in a world where tomorrow was not promised, morality became **negotiable**.

Wartime Affairs Weren't Always Secrets—They Were Sanctioned

In many cultures, especially during long conflicts, affairs were **quietly tolerated** by communities. People looked the other way. Women helped each other hide lovers. Children learned not to ask about "Uncle Joseph."

Even the government turned a blind eye. During World War II, **Allied troops were explicitly told not to judge or interfere with local populations "making arrangements" with soldiers**, especially in places where economic collapse had reduced options to two: **starve or sleep.**

And back home, men wrote letters to wives they hoped were faithful—while visiting brothels or "temporary wives" near the front lines. Infidelity wasn't the exception. **It was the currency of comfort.**

Post-War Pregnancies, Hidden Paternities

One of the most sobering truths of wartime love is what happens after the war. Many women got pregnant by men they didn't marry. By soldiers who disappeared. By enemies they had no intention of loving. And those babies? They came home with last names that didn't match anyone in the family tree.

Entire generations were raised in lies. "Your father died in the war" became a euphemism for "I don't know which man made you." Or worse—"He went back to his country and forgot we existed."

But no one blamed the man. They blamed the mother.

Because wartime morality was a **one-way street**—he was traumatized, she was a whore.

The Return of the Husband—and the Return of the Lie

When soldiers returned, they came back to homes that had changed. Wives had aged. Kids had grown. Neighbors had secrets. And in some cases, **another man had been living there**—in spirit, if not in flesh.

Some men forgave. Some left. Others stayed silent because they had done the same thing on another continent. The mutual betrayal became an **unspoken truce**: "We both did what we had to do."

But many women never confessed. Not because they were ashamed. But because they knew **no one would understand**. That the world only forgives men for infidelity. Women? Never. Even when the bombs were falling.

Love in Wartime Wasn't a Sin. It Was a Response.

To be alive in war is to feel every emotion amplified: love, fear, hunger, lust, grief. And in that chaos, people don't always follow the rules—they follow the **instinct to connect before it's too late**.

Affairs during war weren't always planned. They weren't always passionate. Sometimes they were just **two people clinging to warmth in a frozen world**.

A woman wasn't betraying her husband when she slept with someone while he was at war.

She was **refusing to let herself turn into stone.**

The Truth Nobody Wants to Print on a Medal

Ask any historian who's honest and they'll tell you: wartime cheating was common. Normal. Expected. Sometimes necessary.

But we still romanticize the faithful wife, the brave soldier, the perfect reunion. Because the real story is messy. It makes us uncomfortable. It tells us that even in our most "noble" wars, **we were still animals—hungry, scared, and desperate to be touched.**

So no, wartime cheating wasn't always a moral collapse.

Sometimes it was the **only thing holding a person together**.

And if that offends your fairy tale,

good.

Because history was never made in fairy tales—

it was made in dark rooms, broken hearts, and whispered names we were never supposed to know.

Hollywood and Media Glorification

Films and novels romanticize the mistress and the married lover—shaping modern fantasies.

Adultery, But Make It Beautiful

You're not supposed to root for the mistress. You're not supposed to cheer when the wife gets betrayed. But if you've watched a movie, read a romance novel, or binge-watched a Netflix series in the last fifty years, chances are you've done both—and *felt good about it*.

That's not an accident. That's **storytelling by design**.

Hollywood, literature, music—they've turned infidelity into **aesthetic rebellion**. The mistress isn't a homewrecker—she's *misunderstood*. The married man isn't a liar—he's *torn between two worlds*. The affair isn't a betrayal—it's a *destined, slow-burning, forbidden soul-connection wrapped in rainy kisses and late-night longing*.

And the audience? We eat it up like popcorn at a funeral.

Because deep down, many people don't want to watch healthy, functional, monogamous relationships. They want **desire with consequences**, **love with danger**, and **passion that's too strong to follow the rules**.

Hollywood sells the fantasy. And the fantasy is this:

It's not wrong if it feels this good.

The Mistress as the Main Character

From *The Bridges of Madison County* to *Unfaithful*, from *The English Patient* to *Mad Men*, we've seen it over and over again: the mistress isn't some side character in shame. She's *the star*. She's beautiful. Complicated. Trapped in a world that never deserved her.

And when she falls in love with a married man, we're not disgusted. We're **hooked**.

Why? Because Hollywood reframes the affair as *romantic tragedy*—not selfishness. She's not evil. She's just been waiting her whole life to be seen. He's not an adulterer. He's just a man who found real love too late.

They're *not bad people*—they're just *star-crossed lovers in the wrong timeline*.

And suddenly, betrayal becomes poetic.

Sex becomes salvation.

And the audience—especially women—are left thinking, *Maybe being "the other woman" isn't so shameful after all.*

The Married Man as the Ultimate Fantasy

There's something intoxicating about the married man on screen. He's mature. He's stable. He knows how to speak, how to touch, how to *choose*—even if it's the "wrong" choice.

From *Dr. Zhivago* to *The Affair*, media paints the married man not as a liar, but as a victim of his own passion. He's trapped in a dull marriage. He didn't *mean* to fall in love again. But now that he has, *how could you blame him?*

He's not just a cheater. He's a man pulled in two directions. And the one pulling harder is usually **you**, the mistress. The fantasy isn't just being wanted. It's **being wanted enough to destroy everything for**.

Hollywood doesn't show the broken family, the custody battle, the resentment. It shows the *moment before all of that*—the hotel room. The stolen glance. The clothes on the floor. The first "I can't do this anymore" before they do it again.

Infidelity Becomes a Luxury Brand

Let's be honest. In the media, cheating is rarely shown as messy or pathetic. It's **luxurious**.

They're cheating in Paris. In high-rise penthouses. At art galleries. In limousines. No one's cheating in a trailer park with unpaid bills and morning breath. Infidelity, as sold by media, is *dripping with silk sheets, whispered secrets, and perfectly placed lipstick.*

And women watching? They don't just want the man—they want the *life* that comes with him. The apartment. The champagne. The thrill. The danger. The drama. All of it becomes part of the *package.*

The affair isn't just about sex—it's about **escaping boredom, responsibility, routine**. It's marketed as *freedom.* But only the mistress gets to look free. The wife? She gets wrinkles and laundry.

Why We Love Watching People Ruin Their Lives

Here's the psychological trick: people don't watch these stories because they approve of cheating. They watch them because cheating taps into something that marriage, ironically, often suppresses—**the urgency of desire**.

The forbidden kiss. The impossible love. The risk of everything for one night of meaning. It's cinematic gold. Because people don't just want safety. They want to *feel.* And stories about affairs remind us that **feeling something too deeply might still be better than feeling nothing at all.**

It's not the sex we crave—it's the *significance.*

Affairs are painted as *proof* that passion still matters. That some loves are worth the wreckage.

And media never shows the reality after the credits roll—only the flames just before the crash.

Songs That Made Side Chicks Sing

Let's not forget music.

From Beyoncé's *"Dangerously in Love"* to Alicia Keys' *"Un-Thinkable"*, from SZA's *"The Weekend"* to Brandy and Monica's *"The Boy Is Mine"*, side pieces have been singing **their side of the story for decades.**

They're not hiding. They're harmonizing. And often, they're not ashamed.

These songs frame the mistress not as guilty, but as *in love*. As *chosen*. As *finally heard*. They suggest something most people are too afraid to say: **that being "the other woman" isn't just about sex—it's about finally being someone's obsession.**

And the woman listening to those songs in her car on the way to her 9-to-5? She's not just vibing. She's imagining what it's like to *matter that much*.

From Taboo to Trophy

Once upon a time, being a mistress was a secret, a scandal, a scarlet letter. Now? She's an **archetype**, a style, a story arc. She's the mysterious stranger in black. She's the one who makes him feel alive. She's the one who gets the candlelight while the wife gets the ceiling fan.

And thanks to media, **many women no longer see the mistress as a cautionary tale—but as a challenge. A fantasy. A path.**

Because she's not just the "other woman."

She's the *main character in a story that finally belongs to her*.

The Wife Is Boring. The Mistress Is the Plot.

In most media, the wife is flat. Predictable. Tired. She wants to talk about bills. She nags. She cries.

The mistress? She whispers. She laughs. She vanishes before dawn.

She's not a person—she's a metaphor for everything the man has lost and everything the audience secretly wants: **the thrill of disobedience, the fire of forbidden, the rush of being remembered.**

And that's the real seduction. Not just of the man in the film, but of *you*, the viewer.

You don't want to be the mistress.

You just want to feel like the person people ruin their lives over.

And Hollywood knows that.

And sells it.

Over. And over. And over.

So no, the media didn't invent the mistress.

It just gave her better lighting.

Better lines.
And made her **look like the only honest person in a world of lies.**
Because if love is a battlefield,
the mistress is the soldier who stopped pretending there were rules.
And we?
We're still watching her burn it down—frame by glorious frame.

Chapter 3: The Psychology of the Mistress

Why women accept the mistress role and don't always demand exclusivity

The Lie Everyone Tells: "No Woman Wants to Be the Other Woman"

That's what they say, right? That no woman wants to be second. That every mistress is secretly miserable. That she's deluded, heartbroken, waiting for him to leave his wife like a loyal dog in designer lingerie.

That's the comfort narrative. The one wives tell themselves. The one society repeats. The one movies pretend to resolve with some moral redemption arc.

But reality? Darker. Funnier. Sharper.

Because the truth is this: **many mistresses are not victims of men—they are *choosing* the role**. Not because they have no self-worth. But because they understand the **psychology of the game**, and sometimes? They prefer the shadows.

This chapter isn't about blame. It's about *truth*.

And the truth is, **a lot of women don't want the ring. They want the power that comes with never needing it.**

Control Without Commitment: Why the Mistress Has the Upper Hand

Let's be brutally honest—being a wife is work. It's logistics. It's school schedules and in-laws and joint accounts and morning breath and "we need to talk." It's sex that becomes routine. Love that gets buried under laundry.

The mistress? She gets the curated version.

She gets the cologne, the compliments, the **uninterrupted attention**. She gets him when he's escaping stress, not dumping it.

She doesn't care how he folds the towels.

She cares how he undresses her.

And more importantly? **She controls the clock.**

He comes when she allows. He texts when she wants. She doesn't owe him anything—no holidays, no anniversaries, no explanations. He's the one chasing *her*.

And in a world where so many women are taught to serve, submit, and stay small, the mistress role offers something rare: **psychological leverage.**

Validation Through Exclusivity? Some Women Prefer Validation Through Selectivity

The traditional belief is that women want to be "the one." The only. The forever. But not all women dream of white dresses and exclusive titles. Some women—especially those with **high self-awareness, emotional intelligence, or deep cynicism**—see the world for what it is: *monogamy is not always realistic, and exclusivity is not always desirable.*

For them, being the mistress is about **quality over quantity**. They'd rather have intense, sporadic passion than daily emotional labor. They'd rather be the fantasy than the responsibility.

And while wives often compete to be the *only*, mistresses often settle for being the *most unforgettable*. And guess what? **That's often more intoxicating.**

The Allure of Being Chosen—Over and Over Again

Here's a psychological twist: being chosen *once* in a marriage is fine. Being chosen *every time he cheats*? That's a different kind of power.

Many mistresses know they're not the first. And they know they won't be the last. But they don't need permanence. They need *preference*.

He keeps coming back. He risks discovery. He lies for her. Protects her. Makes excuses for her. That repetitive choosing becomes its own form of validation.

It whispers: *You're the exception.*

You're the addiction.

You're the one he'd rather be with—even if he never fully can.

And for some women, that's more affirming than a diamond on a finger and a man asleep on the couch.

Emotional Safety in Emotional Distance

Not every woman wants to be loved loudly. Some want to be loved *from a distance*—controlled, contained, on their terms.

Mistresses often suffer less emotional risk. She knows what he is. She expects less. She's not banking on forever. So when he fails, she isn't blindsided—she's *prepared.*

Ironically, the mistress may be more emotionally stable than the wife.

The wife gambled everything.

The mistress? She just rolled the dice for fun—and walked away with his soul, not his surname.

The Thrill of Transgression

Let's not ignore the obvious: **for some women, the affair is the turn-on.**

The risk. The secrecy. The knowing smirk in public and the fevered hands in private. The fact that she holds what another woman thinks she owns.

It's not cruelty. It's **erotic rebellion.**

Because nothing screams *I exist on my own terms* like breaking rules and *enjoying* it.

She's not just seducing the man—she's seducing the taboo.

And the louder society tells her "you shouldn't,"

the more her subconscious whispers, *watch me.*

Father Wounds and Fantasy Fulfillment

Now let's go deeper.

Many mistresses—though not all—have experienced **emotional abandonment.** Absent fathers. Unavailable men. Love that came in fragments. And so the married man becomes a familiar shape: *he's present, but only in pieces.*

She tells herself this time will be different. This time, she'll win. This time, he'll choose her permanently.

It's not just an affair. It's **a psychological reenactment**—and this time, she's in control. That's not foolish. That's deeply human. Painful, yes. But also smart. Because she's rewriting the story on *her terms*, even if she knows how it ends.

Being the Secret is Safer Than Being the Wife

Wives are publicly adored. But they're also publicly judged. Criticized. Controlled. Watched. Mistresses? They're invisible. And that invisibility is power.

She doesn't have to play by the rules.

She doesn't have to perform.

She doesn't have to pretend.

She gets to be herself—or at least the best, most liberated version of herself—without the weight of expectation.

Because sometimes, *being the secret is more freeing than being the center.*

Low Investment, High Return: The Economics of Illicit Love

Mistresses often get more with less.

- No legal commitment
- No domestic labor
- No shared debt
- But emotional highs, sexual attention, and the fantasy of being "chosen" again and again.

She didn't marry him. She doesn't clean up after him. But she still gets **his best self**—the one that's charming, apologetic, hungry.

That's a bargain many women—especially those who've *seen what marriage does to desire*—are willing to make.

Jealousy? Sure. But Also Power

Let's not pretend mistresses don't feel jealousy. They do. But many learn to **turn jealousy into fuel**—fuel to compete, to control, to *win in her own way.*

She knows she's not the wife. But the wife can't make him sneak out at midnight. Can't make him lose sleep. Can't make him tremble.

She can.

And in that moment, *she owns him more than a marriage certificate ever could.*

So no, the mistress isn't always a fool.

She isn't always broken.

She isn't waiting for the man to leave.

Sometimes she doesn't even want him to.

Because the truth is, not every woman wants the whole man.

Some are satisfied being the part he can never forget.

And sometimes?

That's more powerful than being the woman he lives with.

Because when he's bored, tired, numb—

He doesn't call the wife.

He calls **her**.

The Allure of the Forbidden

Cheating adds drama and excitement—psychologically addictive feelings.

If It's Wrong, Why Does It Feel So Good?

Because your brain is a drama addict, that's why.

Because nothing makes the heart race faster than what you're not supposed to touch.

Because cheating, forbidden love, secret lust—these things aren't just morally dangerous. They're *biologically engineered to feel like the best drug you've ever taken.*

The allure of the forbidden isn't just about sex. It's about **dopamine**. About **power**. About **the thrill of almost getting caught**. And once you taste that high, a boring, safe, faithful relationship feels like trying to get drunk off a glass of warm milk.

It's not love that makes people cheat. It's **the addiction to emotion**, the adrenaline, the sneaky text message, the locked door, the feeling of doing something so taboo it sets your skin on fire.

And the worst part? Your brain rewards you for it. It lights up like a Christmas tree every time you do something that breaks the rules—and gets away with it.

Forbidden = Valuable

Here's how the brain works: we don't just want what's good. We want what's **scarce**. What's limited. What's risky.

And in relationships, nothing screams "rare treasure" like the **forbidden.**

Married men. Taken women. The boss. The best friend's spouse. The emotionally unavailable wreck who texts "I shouldn't be doing this" at 2:00 AM. These people aren't special.

But because they're **off-limits**, they become **irresistible**.

Your brain says:

"If it's forbidden, it must be important."

"If it's hidden, it must be worth it."

"If I could lose everything for this... then this must be *everything*."

It's the same reason diamonds cost more than glass—**scarcity sells**. Even when it's destructive.

The High-Stakes Hormone Hit

Cheating triggers a biochemical cocktail that makes heroin look polite.

- **Dopamine** floods the brain during risk.
- **Oxytocin** surges during secret intimacy.
- **Adrenaline** spikes during the threat of being caught.
- **Cortisol** adds stress, which makes the eventual release even more intense.

The whole thing becomes a **neurochemical rollercoaster**—pleasure, guilt, secrecy, fear, euphoria—and every loop makes the ride harder to get off.

This is why people stay in affairs that destroy them.

They're not chasing love.

They're chasing the **chemical chaos of forbidden desire**.

Routine Kills. Danger Resurrects.

Monogamy feels safe. But safety isn't sexy.

You know what's sexy? Risk.

- Doing something you're not supposed to.

- Kissing someone in the dark while your phone is blowing up.

- Hearing "you're the only one who makes me feel this alive."

- Slipping out of a dinner party to meet a secret lover two blocks away.

That's not responsible.
That's not stable.
That's not mature.
But it is *electric.*

And for many people stuck in the gray fog of routine, **a single spark of danger feels more alive than a decade of quiet love.**

You're Not in Love—You're in Withdrawal

Here's the most disturbing truth: many people think they're "in love" with the person they're cheating with. But what they're actually experiencing is **chemical dependency**.

It's not the person. It's the process.

The planning. The anticipation. The secrecy. The stolen moments.

The emotional rollercoaster of infidelity mimics **addiction**. And like all addicts, cheaters often **mistake the high for the relationship**.

Then reality hits. The affair gets exposed. The secrecy ends. The thrill fades. And they wonder why the passion evaporated the moment it became *legal.*

Because forbidden love isn't built to last.

It's built to **burn fast and leave scars.**

Why "Getting Caught" Makes It Better—Until It Destroys You

People don't always cheat in secret because they're careful. Sometimes, they **want to be caught**.

The tension of getting close to discovery becomes *part of the thrill.*

It's the emotional equivalent of edging—building tension, skirting the line, getting off on the idea that *everything could collapse any second.*

And when it finally does?

The explosion is almost satisfying.

- The confession.
- The tears.
- The confrontation.
- The chaos.

It's all **more real** than anything they've felt in years.

Because people who cheat aren't just chasing sex.

They're chasing a *plotline.* And sometimes, **destruction is the climax.**

The Secret Keeps It Sacred

You know why affairs often die the second they're exposed?

Because they're not built on reality. They're built on **imagination**.

The hotel room. The whispers. The sneaking around. The dual lives. It all builds a fantasy world that can only exist in the dark.

Once the lights come on? The magic dies.

Suddenly, it's just two flawed people with bad habits and a broken trail behind them.

The mistress becomes clingy.

The married man becomes cowardly.

The thrill becomes burden.

The passion becomes pressure.

Because the **power of the affair isn't just the person—it's the secrecy.**

Women Know This Too—And Some Prefer It That Way

Let's be crystal clear: women aren't just passive players in this game.

Plenty of women knowingly enter affairs not because they're stupid or desperate—but because **they're addicted to the exact same forbidden feeling**.

She doesn't want your boring Tuesday morning affection.

She wants your shaking hands at midnight.

She wants your guilt, your lust, your inability to control yourself.

She wants to feel like she *owns the part of you no one else can have.*

It's not weakness. It's **power, wrapped in lace and lies.**

Cheating Isn't a Mistake. It's a Fix.

Most people don't stumble into infidelity by accident. They drift toward it. They crave it long before it happens.

Because cheating scratches an itch monogamy often ignores:

- The need to feel desired again.
- The need to be chased.
- The need to be a *secret*, not a responsibility.
- The need to feel *something other than numb.*

And once they taste it, most don't want the affair to become a relationship.

They want it to stay forbidden—because **that's what makes it worth doing**.

So no, cheating doesn't happen because someone stopped loving their partner.

It happens because **forbidden love tastes sweeter than loyalty ever could.**

Not because it's right.

But because *your brain doesn't care about right.*

It cares about **what makes your heart race while your life collapses quietly in the background.**

Low Commitment, High Reward

Some women prefer limited emotional investment with material or emotional gains.

Not Every Woman Wants the Whole Man

Here's the myth you've been sold: every woman wants a ring, a husband, a mortgage, and the long, slow march toward joint funerals.

Here's the truth too many are afraid to admit: **some women want exactly the opposite.**

They don't want full-time love. They want **part-time power.**

They don't want the entire man. They want **the version of him who's generous, attentive, desperate, and *just out of reach.***

And if she can get that—without folding his laundry, raising his kids, or listening to him snore—**why wouldn't she?**

In a world where emotional labor is unpaid and devotion is often unrewarded, *being the mistress is sometimes the smartest role in the entire romantic economy.*

Low commitment.

High reward.

Minimal bullshit.

The Business Model of Infidelity: Supply, Demand, and Selective Investment

Think like an economist. Marriage is a full-time job with poor benefits, questionable hours, and no guarantees. Being a mistress? That's freelance work with **high compensation and personal autonomy.**

She doesn't cook his meals—he takes her to dinner.

She doesn't nag him—she gets his undivided attention.

She doesn't pay the bills—he buys her gifts, covers rent, sends GCash.

She doesn't ask for fidelity—she asks for a new iPhone.

This isn't manipulation. It's **efficiency**.

She's doing the emotional math:

"How little do I have to give to get what I want?"

And often, the answer is: **very little**.

Freedom with Perks

The beauty of low-commitment relationships is freedom. The ability to vanish, to detach, to skip the drama and come back when the vibe is right. Mistress arrangements often allow a woman to enjoy:

- *Attention without attachment*
- *Sex without expectations*
- *Gifts without guilt*
- *Intimacy without entrapment*

She gets the fire *without the contract.*

The affection *without the obligation*.

And if he cheats on his wife to be with her, she knows the rulebook: **she's not next—she's optional**.

And that's exactly how she wants it.

She Doesn't Want His Love. She Wants His Obsession—In Controlled Doses

Love is messy. Demanding. Suffocating.

Obsession, though? Obsession is manageable—**if it's not yours**.

Some women *don't* want to be in love. They've seen what it does.

They've watched friends fall apart. They've been the wife. They've read the fairytales and burned them.

So instead, they take a man who's already taken—and **they control the narrative.**

She doesn't cry if he forgets a date.

She doesn't need to impress his family.

She doesn't care what his kids think.

She just wants to be the thought that ruins his focus, the reason he hesitates before going home.

That's not weakness. That's strategy.

Emotional ROI: Relationships with a Profit Margin

Not all women are romantics. Some are **realists with sharp intuition and even sharper spreadsheets**. They track the emotional return on investment like a Wall Street broker.

- A full-time boyfriend requires emotional upkeep.
- A husband demands devotion, sacrifice, patience.
- A lover? He shows up, spoils her, leaves.

She's not investing in "forever." She's investing in *now*—and cashing out when the market dips.

And if she gets Chanel, rent money, a trip to El Nido, and a guilt-fueled text that says "you're the only one I can talk to"... that's **more reward than most wives get in five years.**

Some Women Don't Want the Drama. They Want the Edge.

Not every mistress is an emotional wreck. Some are **cool, calculated, and completely in control**. They're not falling for promises. They're collecting leverage.

- They don't stalk the wife's Instagram.
- They don't wait by the phone.
- They don't fantasize about being chosen.

They know exactly what this is: **a transaction with emotional flair.**

They play the part. Moan at the right moment. Send the risky selfie. Pull back just enough to keep him chasing. Then go home and sleep soundly knowing they're not the one stuck cleaning his skid-marked boxers or hearing him snore after pork sinigang.

She has him on the weekends.

She has her own life on weekdays.

She doesn't share a bed. She shares a spell.

He Pays in Guilt. She Banks in Benefits.

One of the most overlooked dynamics in the mistress-man relationship is this: **his guilt is her goldmine**.

He buys her things not because she asks—but because *he's trying to quiet his conscience.*

He gives her time, money, and affection because *he knows he's wrong.*

And that moral imbalance? It becomes her **leverage**.

She never needs to threaten. She just needs to exist.

Because every moment he spends with her is a moment stolen.

And every stolen moment feels more valuable than a hundred honest ones.

She's not deluded.

She's **profiting from his internal collapse**.

Some Women Have Already Had the Marriage—and Don't Want It Again

Mistresses aren't always young, naive, or in need. Many are **divorced, experienced, emotionally self-sufficient** women who've *been there, done that, got the heartbreak.*

They don't want another husband.

They want autonomy, attention, and just enough intimacy to keep their souls warm—but never trapped.

Being a mistress is a conscious, curated role:

- No joint taxes.
- No shared responsibilities.
- No long-term negotiations.

Just desire, distance, and the occasional soft lie whispered against her neck.

She knows the script. She doesn't expect him to leave his wife.

In fact, she *prefers that he doesn't.*

The Wife Holds His Name. The Mistress Holds His Mind.

Society loves to say the wife wins. She gets the house, the kids, the family name. But ask yourself: **what part of the man does she actually get?**

The bored part. The tired part. The silent, distracted, emotionally unavailable part.

The mistress? She gets the part that *feels.*

The part that's still curious, still alive, still wild.

The part that remembers how to want.

And some women are satisfied being the *voice in his head* rather than the name on his tax returns.

So no, not every woman wants "the whole thing."

Some just want *what matters most.*

Not his heart. Not his last name.

Just the version of him he never shows anyone else.

And in this rigged game of love, marriage, and betrayal—

Sometimes **she's the only one playing to win.**

Avoidance of Intimacy

A mistress role provides love without the burdens of marriage or household responsibilities.

Some Women Don't Want Intimacy—They Want Intensity in Small, Controlled Doses

Let's murder another myth: not all women are out here dreaming of emotional closeness, shared toothbrush holders, and deeply vulnerable late-night talks about the future.

Some women don't want closeness. They want **control**.

And ironically, becoming a mistress gives them exactly that.

She doesn't want the mess of intimacy. The daily grind of relationships. The morning breath, the passive-aggressive silences, the "we need to talk" moments that last for hours.

She wants the **edited version of connection**—the emotional equivalent of a highlight reel. Passion without paperwork. Affection without accountability. A man who feels, touches, craves—but always *leaves before it gets too real.*

This isn't coldness. This is **surgical self-preservation**.

And the mistress role? It's the perfect armor.

A Lover You Don't Have to Live With

Living with someone sounds romantic—until you've done it.

Until you've seen the socks on the floor, the weaponized silence, the fridge full of expired groceries and empty apologies. That's intimacy. That's the unsexy reality nobody posts on Instagram.

Some women know that. And they want no part of it.

So they choose the mistress role not because they want less love—but because they want **less exposure**.

She sees him for two hours, perfectly dressed, cologned, and ready to impress.

She doesn't see him picking his nose, ignoring her feelings, or losing his job and blaming everyone but himself.

She gets the best of him—**without having to share a home, a bathroom, or a tax form.**

Love Without Laundry

Here's the brutal math of traditional relationships:

- Emotional connection = commitment
- Commitment = daily responsibility
- Daily responsibility = fatigue, friction, routine
- Routine = death of desire

The mistress sidesteps that entire equation.

She doesn't clean his shirts. She doesn't raise his kids. She doesn't share his debt, his dishes, or his demons.

And in doing so, she **keeps the illusion alive**. The illusion that love can stay light, seductive, mysterious—if you just never have to manage someone's life.

This is what people don't get: **the mistress often has deeper emotional self-awareness than the wife.** She knows the cost of closeness. She's felt the weight of "forever." She's not escaping responsibility—she's *selecting boundaries.*

She Wants Touch, Not Tethers

We are trained to believe that physical connection must lead to emotional intimacy. That if a woman gives her body, she wants to give her soul too.

But the truth is—many women crave physical affection without the psychological entanglement.

They want to feel wanted, worshipped, adored... without having to be vulnerable every single day.

They want to be loved—but **not consumed.**

The mistress gets that.

She's loved when she wants it.

She disappears when she doesn't.

And no one expects her to show up on Monday morning ready to talk about bills and future goals.

It's not selfish. It's survival.

Some Women Know That "Real Intimacy" Comes with a Body Count

Real intimacy means revealing the ugliest parts of yourself. The insecurities. The trauma. The habits that repel affection. The rage. The silence. The fear.

Not everyone can do that.

And some women—burned by betrayal, abandonment, childhood trauma, or simply **the exhaustion of being deeply known and deeply hurt**—decide: *Never again.*

So they choose the mistress role. Because it allows them to **stay close enough to feel alive, but far enough to never feel exposed.**

It's a safe zone. A holding pattern. A strategic compromise between loneliness and destruction.

And they're not wrong. For many, it works.

She Doesn't Want the Whole Man—She Wants the Version That Doesn't Hurt Her

The married man she's sleeping with?

He's curated. Tamed. On his best behavior. He doesn't explode. He doesn't blame. He doesn't expect emotional labor.

Why? Because he knows he can't.

She's not trapped. He is.

And that gives her the freedom to **enjoy a man without absorbing his chaos.**

She gets the parts of him that are sweet, seductive, and hungry—and she avoids the parts that ruin lives.

That's not a lack of intimacy. That's **intimacy on her terms.**

Why Be a Wife When You Can Be the Fever?

Wives get security.

Mistresses get memory.

Wives get bedtime routines.

Mistresses get 2AM confessions and trembling hands.

Wives get "we'll talk about it tomorrow."

Mistresses get "I can't stop thinking about you."

Some women don't want the man who stays.

They want the man who *aches.*

Who *chases.*

Who *loses sleep thinking about them.*

That's not emotional detachment. That's emotional minimalism—**loving without losing yourself.**

The Avoidant Attachment Queen

Psychology calls it "avoidant attachment."

Society calls it "emotionally unavailable."

She calls it **"I've learned my lesson."**

This is the woman who's seen too much.

She knows what happens when you open your heart like a door—someone walks in with muddy feet and leaves you to clean up the mess.

So now? She keeps the door cracked.

Lets someone peek in. Touch the walls.

But never, ever stays long enough for them to unpack their baggage.

It's not that she's afraid of love.

It's that she's afraid of what love **demands**: total access, total surrender, and *zero protection.*

The Mistress Isn't Weak. She's Surgical.
She slices the relationship into clean, manageable pieces.

- A night of passion.
- A week of silence.
- A message at midnight.
- A dinner she controls.

She never gets lost in it. She never drowns.

She lets herself feel just enough to stay warm—but never enough to burn.

And for many women? That's the **only safe way to love.**

So no, the mistress role isn't always about competing with the wife.

Sometimes it's about **avoiding the very thing the wife suffers under**—daily, invasive, emotionally exhausting intimacy.

She doesn't want to share a life.

She just wants to **taste one that doesn't swallow her whole**.

And sometimes? That's the wisest love of all.

Validation and Competition

"Winning" a man from another woman boosts ego and self-worth.

This Isn't About Him. It's About *Her Winning*

Let's make this brutally clear from the jump: many mistresses don't actually want the man. They want the *victory*. The affirmation. The psychological trophy that says, *"I am better than the woman he committed to."*

It's not about love. It's not about soulmates. It's not even about lust half the time.

It's about **ego.**

Because when a woman takes a man who already belongs to someone else, she's not just sleeping with him—she's **defeating her**.

This is the kind of dark, delicious competition no one talks about at brunch but everyone secretly understands.

You're not just the other woman.

You're the **woman she couldn't outcompete**.

You're the *exception*.

When Another Woman's Man Chooses You—You Win the Game Society Designed

Let's be real: women are trained from birth to **compete for male attention.** It's built into culture, media, fashion, religion, and every Disney movie that taught little girls to fight for Prince Charming—even if he was emotionally constipated and had the personality of a wet sponge.

And in that game, taking a man from another woman isn't cheating—it's *winning on hard mode.*

If he's single, anyone can have him.

But if he's married or taken?

And he still texts you "I can't stop thinking about you"?

Then you must be something *extraordinary.*

The forbidden becomes a mirror.

And in that mirror, you don't see shame—you see superiority.

"If He Cheats With Me, I Must Be Better Than Her"

Here's where it gets disturbingly honest.

A lot of women don't want to be *a* woman in a man's life—they want to be *the one he risks everything for.* The one who pulls him away from stability. The one who makes him *choose against his own vows.*

Not because she's evil. But because she's *starving for proof that she is desirable, powerful, and unforgettable.*

And in a world where women are constantly devalued, ignored, or replaced, **stealing someone else's man becomes a twisted form of self-worth**.

She's not thinking, "He's a liar."

She's thinking, *"If I were her, I'd hate me too."*

And that hate feels like victory.

The Other Woman Is Just the Background Character

Once the affair begins, the wife or girlfriend becomes a shadow.

A name. A fact.

But never a *threat.*

Because in the mistress's mind, if he was truly happy, truly fulfilled, truly satisfied—he wouldn't be here, naked and begging in *her* bed.

The existence of the other woman stops being sacred.

It becomes *evidence of superiority.*

Every time he lies to his wife to see his mistress, she gets a psychological payout:

- "He chose me."
- "He escaped her for me."
- "She keeps the marriage. I keep the part of him that's still alive."

This Is Predator vs. Prey—and It's Not Always the Man Who's the Hunter

Don't underestimate the *sport* of infidelity.

Some women enjoy the chase. Not of the man—but of the status boost that comes with *stealing someone else's "secure" partner.*

They see the wife as complacent.

They see the girlfriend as basic.

They see themselves as *evolved*—capable of unlocking a man's primal need to escape domestic mediocrity.

They're not seducing for sex.

They're seducing for *dominance.*

And every time he texts, "I miss you," she hears:

"You win again."

The Mistress Role as a Mirror for Insecurity

Of course, this isn't always confidence.

Sometimes, it's the exact opposite.

Some women need constant proof that they are worthy. That they are desirable. That they are still *wanted.*

And what better proof than a man **risking his marriage just to be near you?**

It's sick validation.

But it *feels* real.

- He leaves her bed to call you.
- He buys you gifts he doesn't buy his wife.

- He texts you "I love you" from the bathroom while his family eats dinner.

You might hate yourself in the morning.

But for those few hours?

You feel like *a goddess made of gasoline and broken rules.*

Why Public Women Fall for Married Men

It's not always the side chick. Sometimes it's the CEO. The influencer. The self-made woman who has everything—except the **emotional confirmation** that she's still desirable, irreplaceable, unforgettable.

So she takes what society says she shouldn't.

And when that married man melts in her hands, she doesn't feel immoral.

She feels *validated.*

Because power isn't just being wanted—it's being wanted **more than someone society says he's supposed to love.**

Even If He Never Leaves Her—She Still Won

One of the most tragicomic truths of this dynamic is this: **he can stay married and she still feels victorious.**

Because in her mind, the affair is the *proof.*

He didn't have to ruin his life. He just had to **sneak away to her arms to remember what it feels like to want again.**

And when he goes back to his wife, to the normalcy, to the routine, she smiles.

Because he's going back to a role.

But she?

She's the *escape from that role.*

She's the fire he touches when he's sure no one's watching.

It's Not About Love. It's About Beating Her.

That's the secret.

The affair is never just between two people.

There's always a *third woman in the room*—and she doesn't even have to be there. Her existence alone makes it a **competition.**

And when the mistress wins—even temporarily—she *feels* it in her bones.

Every moan. Every message. Every "I wish I met you before I married her" becomes a point on the scoreboard.

She doesn't want the man.

She wants **the proof that she's better than the woman who got him first**.

So no, it's not just about love.

It's not just about sex.

Sometimes?

It's about *revenge on the world for ever making her feel second best.*

And now that she's the one being chased, devoured, chosen—

She finally feels like enough.

Even if it's borrowed.

Even if it's broken.

Even if it only lasts one unforgettable night at a time.

Fantasy vs. Reality

The mistress lives in the fantasy—she sees the best of him, not the everyday struggles.

She's Not in Love with the Man—She's in Love with the Version of Him That Only Exists in Secret

Let's start here: the man the mistress knows is not the man he *really is*—he's the **edited version**. The trailer, not the full movie. The highlight reel, not the blooper reel. The version that shows up clean, smooth-talking, desperate, and charming—because *he only exists in moments.*

She gets the man who escapes.

The one who's running *from* responsibility, not carrying it.

The man who opens doors, plans dates, whispers promises—but doesn't snore, doesn't stress, doesn't sulk.

She gets the *fantasy.*

Because the fantasy is all she's allowed to see.

The Wife Lives With the Beast. The Mistress Gets the Mask.

The wife sees it all.

She knows how impatient he gets with the kids.

She knows the bills he hides and the drinking he downplays.

She's watched him fail, fall apart, lose his cool, shut down, numb out.

The mistress? She gets two hours of curated charisma.

She doesn't see the temper. She doesn't see the apathy.

She sees the *performance.*

The version of him that's been washed in guilt, sprayed with cologne, and lit by the glow of forbidden lust.

It's not real. It's not even *close* to real.

But that's the point—**reality doesn't sell. Fantasy does.**

When You Only See Someone at Their Best, You Think That's Who They Are

It's easy to fall in love with a man who never shares a bank account with you.

Who never farts next to you in bed.

Who never judges your stretch marks, ignores your anxiety, or forgets your birthday.

The mistress only knows **the man he wants to be**, not the man he is when no one's watching.

She falls in love with the illusion:

- That he's romantic.
- That he's gentle.
- That he's emotionally deep.
- That he'd be different if they were "free."

Spoiler: he wouldn't.

Because when the affair becomes the relationship, the fantasy collapses like a stage set hit by a hurricane.

The flowers stop.

The good sex turns into silent dinners.

The passion fades—and suddenly she realizes she never loved the man.

She loved the **escape**.

The Affair Is a Movie. Marriage Is the Behind-the-Scenes Documentary.

Affairs come with music, mood lighting, tension, urgency.

Marriage comes with dishes, doctor visits, diapers, and depression.

In an affair, every moment is *chosen*. It's stolen time. It's adrenaline. It's heat.

In a marriage, the moments are mundane. Long. Repetitive. Sometimes beautiful. Often exhausting.

The mistress never sees the man fold under pressure.

Never sees him shrink under failure.

Never hears him admit he's scared, broke, or bored with life.

She sees him when he's at his most **alive.**

And so she believes *this is the real him.*

It's not.

It's the version of him *that only exists because he doesn't have to stay.*

She Gets the Poetry. The Wife Gets the Prose.

The man sends the mistress long texts about how he can't stop thinking about her.

About how he feels seen, desired, alive.

He shows up in suits. Says the right things. Orders the right wine. Touches her like it's the first time, every time.

Meanwhile, his wife is dealing with a man who forgot to buy milk.

Who barely listens. Who zones out. Who hasn't said "you look beautiful" in six months.

To the mistress, he's a mystery.

To the wife, he's a routine.

But here's the dark punchline: **the routine is the truth**.

The mystery is the myth.

And once you make the myth your reality, it dies in your hands.

The Mistress Mistakes Attention for Devotion

In the affair, he makes time. Sends messages. Cancels plans. Says "I'd leave for you."

But attention is not devotion.

It's not commitment.

It's not showing up when you're tired, broke, or grieving.

He's not sacrificing. He's indulging.

And the mistress, often desperate to believe she *means something*, mistakes **his distraction from his life** as **loyalty to her**.

But he's not loyal.

He's just running from himself.

And she happens to be a safe place to hide.

He's Performing for Her Because He's Failing Somewhere Else

Most men don't cheat because they're oversexed or underloved.

They cheat because they feel powerless.

Like failures.

Like ghosts in their own homes.

So when the mistress makes them feel desired again, competent again, sexy again—it's like a drug.

And like all addicts, they perform. They become the man they wish they were.

Not because they love her—but because they **hate who they've become everywhere else.**

She's not his new beginning.

She's his **mirror**—reflecting back the man he wants to believe he still is.

And She Believes It. Because She Has to.

If the mistress admits he's lying, posturing, performing—then the fantasy dies.

And with it, the entire foundation of the affair crumbles.

So she chooses the illusion.

She believes he's trapped. That he wants to leave. That she's the exception, not the pattern.

She believes this because **the fantasy is the only thing keeping her from realizing she's just another escape route**.

She Doesn't Want His Whole Life. She Wants the Slice That Tastes the Sweetest

Mistresses often say: "I don't want to ruin his life. I just want my time."

Translation: "I want the part of him that's still passionate, still exciting, still *mine*—and I don't care who has the rest."

It's not selfish.

It's survival.

Because the minute he becomes fully hers, he becomes **just another man who doesn't deliver**.

And the fantasy fades.

So no, she's not in love with *him*.

She's in love with the **edited, airbrushed, curated version of him that can only exist in stolen moments**.

And the tragedy isn't that she'll lose him.

The tragedy is that if she ever *gets* him,

she'll finally meet the man his wife has known all along—

and wonder how she ever fell for the illusion.

Broken Father Figures and Repetition Compulsion

Women with unstable male role models may unconsciously recreate betrayal cycles.

She's Not Dating the Married Man. She's Dating Her Father in Disguise.

This isn't about the sex. It's not about the man.

It's about the pattern.

For some women, stepping into the role of "the other woman" isn't a rebellion—it's a **repetition**.

A tragic, psychological loop.

A rerun of a show they didn't write but somehow can't stop watching.

Because for many mistresses, the affair is not their first betrayal—it's their *latest*.

And the original betrayal? It didn't start with a lover.

It started with **Dad**.

Not always abusive. Not always absent.

Sometimes just emotionally unavailable.

Sometimes just inconsistent.

Sometimes just *there*, but never fully **present**.

And when you grow up learning that the man you love will eventually disappear, lie, or disappoint you—your brain decides: *This is love. This is normal. This is home.*

Daddy Never Came Home—So She Chases Men Who Never Can Stay

The psychology is viciously poetic.

Her father was late. Distant. Preoccupied. Or worse, made her feel invisible unless she worked for his attention.

So now, she finds herself attracted to men who are **emotionally inaccessible.**

Men who belong to someone else.

Men who come in fragments—like her father did.

Because somewhere deep in her subconscious, she's not trying to fall in love.

She's trying to **finally win the attention of the man who couldn't or wouldn't give it to her when it mattered most.**

She's trying to repair what she didn't break.

She's trying to prove she's worthy.

She's trying to rewrite the script with a different ending.

But the roles never change.

He leaves.

She stays.

And the story repeats.

Repetition Compulsion: The Mind's Most Cruel Joke

Freud called it repetition compulsion.

Modern psychology calls it trauma bonding.

Whatever you call it, it's the same sick phenomenon: **we unconsciously recreate the emotional wounds of our childhood in adulthood—not because we enjoy them, but because we want to control the outcome.**

The logic is twisted but real:

- *If I can win this emotionally distant man, I'll finally heal my father wound.*

- *If this married man chooses me, it'll prove I'm lovable.*

- *If I can endure this betrayal, maybe this time it won't destroy me.*

Of course, it always does.

But that's the trap.

The pain feels **familiar**.

And familiarity, for a trauma survivor, *feels like safety.*

She Doesn't Want Chaos—She's Just Addicted to What She's Always Known

Let's kill the judgment right now.

A mistress raised by a broken father doesn't want to be hurt.

She's not seeking suffering.

She's seeking *recognition*—the internal feeling that says, *this pain makes sense, because I've felt it before.*

She's not masochistic.

She's programmed.

Her emotional GPS is malfunctioning—forever guiding her back to places that look like home but feel like hell.

And when you've grown up walking on eggshells around the first man you ever loved, sleeping with someone else's husband doesn't feel wrong.

It feels **familiar.**

She's Not Competing With the Wife—She's Competing With Her Younger Self

It's never about the current relationship.

It's about the one that never healed.

The mistress is trying to win. Not the man—but the *validation she was robbed of as a child.*

She wants to finally feel like *she matters more than someone else.*

Because maybe Dad cheated.

Maybe Dad left.

Maybe Dad chose work, alcohol, or a new family over her.

And now she has a chance to **be the chosen one**—even if the stakes are morally murky, emotionally messy, and guaranteed to end in wreckage.

That risk is nothing compared to the pain she already survived.

Sabotage Disguised as Seduction

Here's the sickest twist: some women cheat with taken men not to win—but to **prove they will always lose**.

They aren't playing to be loved. They're playing to be **abandoned again**—to confirm the belief that they are unworthy, replaceable, not good enough.

It's not conscious.

It's not logical.

But it's psychologically airtight.

- If he stays, she panics.
- If he cheats but never leaves his wife, she says, "See? I knew I didn't deserve more."
- If he promises to leave and doesn't, it replays her father's empty promises word for word.

She's not addicted to men.

She's addicted to **pain that feels like home**.

The Mistress Role Offers Just Enough Love to Stay—And Just Enough Pain to Feel Real

For a woman with a father wound, *healthy love can feel boring*. Safe love can feel fake.

But the mistress role? It offers the **exact emotional cocktail her nervous system was raised on**:

- Partial affection
- Occasional intimacy

- Long stretches of waiting
- Moments of ecstasy
- And deep, hollow drops of disappointment

That's what her childhood felt like.

So of course, that's what her romantic relationships feel like now.

She's not wrong for wanting love.

She's just using a broken compass to find it.

"Maybe This Time I'll Be Enough"

That's the anthem of the mistress with father wounds.

She doesn't want to destroy a marriage.

She wants to finally believe she's *worth staying for.*

Worth choosing.

Worth *betraying someone else for*, because no one ever betrayed their comfort for her.

She doesn't want stolen time.

She wants stolen validation.

She wants the moment he says, "I choose you over everything."

Even if she knows he's lying.

Because hearing the lie is still better than facing the silence of her childhood.

She's Not a Sinner. She's a Survivor in a Broken Pattern.

Mistresses with broken father figures aren't immoral.

They're *injured.*

And like all injuries left untreated, they bleed into every part of life—including who they love, how they love, and how much pain they're willing to tolerate just to feel something close to acceptance.

So no, she's not ruining marriages because she's heartless.

She's revisiting wounds that never closed.

She's not chasing men.

She's chasing **a version of her childhood where she finally gets chosen**.

And until she breaks that cycle,
the man may change,
the story may shift,
but the ending will always be the same:
She's left waiting for a man who never really belonged to her—
just like she once waited for a father who never truly showed up.

Desire for Rescue or Transformation

Some women believe they can change or "heal" the cheater—a romanticized savior complex.

She Doesn't Just Want the Man—She Wants the *Project*

He's emotionally unavailable. He lies. He cheats. He avoids confrontation. He's addicted to control, attention, or sometimes actual substances.

Perfect.

She sees potential.

Because for a certain kind of woman, nothing triggers the heart harder than a **broken man who shows just enough softness to suggest he can be saved.**

And when he's already taken—already "damaged," already deep in deception—**her savior complex kicks in like adrenaline to an EMT.**

She's not just the other woman.

She's the one who believes she was *sent* to change him.

She Doesn't Want the Perfect Man—She Wants to Be the Reason He Becomes One

The fantasy isn't that he's flawless.

It's that *he's flawed for everyone else*—but *becomes better for her.*

He was distant with his wife.

But now he opens up with *her.*

He never talked about his past before.

But with *her*, he's vulnerable.

He never left anyone before.

But this time, she thinks, *he might.*

It's not love. It's a mission.

She wants to *save* him.

Because saving him isn't just about him—it's about **validating her own worth as a woman who can fix the unfixable**.

And if he changes for her?

Then *she wins.*

Not just the man—but the ultimate emotional jackpot: *proof that she matters more than every woman who failed before her.*

The Romantic Lie That Women Are Taught Early

Every little girl is fed a deadly fairytale:

> "He's not bad—he's just misunderstood. And if you love him hard enough, he'll stop being a monster and become a man."

Beauty and the Beast.

Twilight.

Fifty Shades of Gaslighting.

Over and over, we see the story:

The dangerous man is *special.*

He's hurting.

He's a storm.

But with enough love—*he'll transform.*

And this cultural myth turns into emotional reflex.

So when a woman meets a cheater, a liar, a broken mirror of a man—**she sees potential instead of poison**.

She thinks:

> "He just hasn't met someone worth changing for."
> "He's cheating because he's scared—not because he's selfish."
> "I'm not just a lover. I'm his lifeline."

And just like that, the affair becomes a **redemption story she casts herself in.**

She's Not Being Played—She's Playing Therapist

The problem is, she doesn't know she's in a triangle.

She thinks she's in a *rescue narrative.*

The wife is the past. The pain. The prison.

She? She's the healing. The hope. The fresh start.

Every time he vents about how "miserable" he is at home, how "cold" his wife is, how "trapped" he feels—**she steps into the role society programmed her to perform: the woman who saves him from himself.**

It doesn't matter if he never leaves.

As long as he keeps confessing, she keeps *believing.*

Because those confessions don't just bond them—they **bind her self-worth to the illusion that she's changing him**.

This Isn't Love. It's Emotional Codependency in a Sexy Dress

When she builds her identity around rescuing him, she's not in love.

She's addicted to the role of **emotional savior**.

And every setback—every lie, every broken promise—doesn't break the illusion.

It *strengthens* it.

- "He's scared, that's why he lied."
- "He's confused, not cruel."
- "He's not ready yet, but he will be."

The more he hurts her, the more she doubles down.

Because walking away would mean admitting that love **can't** fix someone who doesn't want to change.

And that truth? Too terrifying to face.

She's Not Naive. She's Hopeful to the Point of Self-Destruction

This isn't a stupid woman. This is a deeply *hopeful* woman.

A woman who has likely spent her life believing that her love has to be *proven* through pain.

That the more she suffers for a man, the more he will realize what she's worth.

That if she just *holds on long enough*, the story will turn in her favor.

But here's the real plot twist: **he doesn't want to be saved.**

He wants to be comforted, enabled, adored—**but not transformed.**

Because transformation requires accountability. And most cheaters?

They *excel* at avoiding that.

He Says "You Make Me Want to Be a Better Man." He Doesn't Mean It.

That line? It's classic.

He says it in the dark, hand on her waist, eyes full of regret.

And she believes it.

Because she *needs* to.

Because she's already made the emotional investment.

Because if he doesn't mean it, then what was all this for?

But the truth is, **wanting to be better is not the same as becoming better.**

He wants *relief*, not reform.

He wants *nurturing*, not growth.

He wants *forgiveness*, not change.

And she keeps giving it—because the fantasy isn't that he's perfect.

It's that **she is the one woman capable of pulling perfection out of him.**

If She Saves Him, She Redeems Herself

Here's the deep cut: many women with a savior complex are carrying their own emotional wounds.

They weren't saved.

They weren't protected.

They were let down, forgotten, overlooked.

So now, they pour themselves into *fixing someone else*—believing that if they heal him, they'll heal **themselves.**

That's the trap.

Because no man, no matter how broken or beautiful, can ever repair what another man destroyed.

Especially if he's repeating the same damage.

She Doesn't Want a Man. She Wants a Miracle

And that's the saddest part.

She's not in the affair for the sex, the thrill, or even the stolen moments.

She's in it because she's chasing a miracle.

The miracle that says: *my love is strong enough to change a liar into a loyal man*.

But love doesn't work that way.

It never has.

And by the time she realizes it, the damage is done.

So no, she's not just "the other woman."

She's the *heroine* in a story she wrote in childhood—

where pain was proof, sacrifice was virtue, and redemption was just one more heartbreak away.

And when it all falls apart?

She won't just lose him.

She'll lose the fantasy that **she was ever strong enough to change the ending.**

Chapter 4: The Married Man Magnet

Why women are drawn specifically to married men

He's Already Taken—Which Makes Him Even More Tantalizing

Let's rip the band-aid off: some women don't see the ring as a stop sign. They see it as a **spotlight**.

Because the married man isn't just *unavailable*—he's *validated.*

He's been pre-approved by another woman. Which means, in the twisted market of modern attraction, **he comes with a warranty**.

Some women don't want to test-drive an unclaimed car.

They want the model *someone else already bought, parked in the driveway, and trusted enough to build a family with.*

He's seasoned. He's stable. He knows what to say, how to say it, and when to pretend like he means it.

And for women who've been burned by flaky, commitment-phobic single men who ghost after three dates and a dry kiss, the married man doesn't seem like the villain.

He seems like **the upgrade**.

He Has What She Secretly Wants—Without Demanding That She Pretend to Want the Whole Package

Here's the secret: most women don't actually want the burden of the whole man. They want the curated version. The version that smells like aftershave, says "you're beautiful" like he means it, and texts in full sentences.

The married man? He's emotionally trained.

- He knows how to communicate (because he's had to).
- He knows how to apologize (even if it's fake).
- He knows how to listen (or at least act like it).

He doesn't make the same awkward mistakes as single guys. He doesn't need to be taught. **He's already been domesticated—she just gets to enjoy the benefits.**

She doesn't have to raise him.

She just has to *distract him*.

And that's much less exhausting than trying to build a man from scratch.

The Ring Is a Signal—This Man Has Value

Women live in a brutal dating market. Men who are single are often single for a reason: emotionally unavailable, underemployed, immature, or just flat-out awful in bed.

But a man who's married?

That means another woman looked at him and thought, *Yes, I want to deal with this man every day until death or resentment do us part.*

It's not always logical—but it's **psychologically potent**.

If someone else *wants him*, then **he must be worth something**.

It's called **mate choice copying**—and it's real.

Animals do it. Humans just do it in heels.

He's Confident—Because He Has Nothing to Lose (Until He Does)

Married men carry themselves differently.

They're not needy. They're not chasing. They're not sweating over Tinder matches or DM replies.

They're relaxed. Confident. Sometimes arrogant.

Why? Because they're already "chosen." They're not playing to win.

They're playing because *they're bored*.

And that confidence? That low-key swagger that says "I'm not desperate for you"?

It's catnip.

Especially for women who've only dealt with men who fumble at hello.

The married man doesn't stutter.

He *smolders.*

And he doesn't ask for much—just time, secrecy, and your willingness to ignore the fact that his wife is putting the kids to bed while he's whispering filth into your ear.

He's a Walking Fantasy Because Reality Isn't Her Responsibility

Let's be real—he's attractive *because* he's not available.

Because the relationship is never full-time, it never has to be real.

No bills. No kids. No shared responsibilities. No daily tedium.

Just passion, urgency, and the illusion that he's trapped in a loveless marriage and *you're the cure.*

And that illusion? It's addictive.

Because it feels like a **romantic rebellion**, even when it's just plain old cheating.

You don't have to meet his friends.

You don't have to deal with his mother.

You don't even have to know how annoying he is on weekends.

You just get the man who walks in like sin and makes you feel like a secret worth hiding.

He's Emotionally Complicated—Which Feels Like Depth

Some women mistake emotional unavailability for emotional *depth.*

And the married man plays this role perfectly.

He's torn. He's conflicted. He says things like:

- "I never meant for this to happen."
- "You're the only one who understands me."
- "I haven't felt this alive in years."

And she believes it—not because she's dumb, but because it **feels true in the moment**.

She thinks:

> "If he's risking his marriage to be with me, it must be real."
> What she doesn't see is that **he's not risking anything**—
> He's just rehearsing the same script he's used a dozen times before.

The Drama Feels Like Love

Love isn't always soft. Sometimes it's fire.

And for women raised on chaos, or addicted to emotional highs and lows, the married man provides a **perfect hit of drama**.

- Will he leave her?
- Will he get caught?
- Does he really love me, or am I just a fling?

These questions don't push her away.

They *pull her in*.

Because the uncertainty creates emotional stakes.

And when she's used to love being painful, confusing, and complicated—the married man feels **like home**.

The Guilt Makes the Intimacy Feel Deeper

He's married. He's cheating. He knows it's wrong.

So when he shows up anyway, it feels like a *confession*—a form of intimacy that says:

> "I can't stay away from you."
> "You must be worth it."
> "You must be different."

That guilt he carries? It's **part of the seduction**.

It makes the connection feel sacred. Urgent. Forbidden.

And the more it feels like a sin, the more she believes it must be love.

Because why else would someone **risk their whole life** just to be near you?

She Thinks She's Special—Because He Treats Her Like the Exception

This is the cruelest part:

He tells her she's different.

He tells her he's never done this before.

He tells her *he's thinking about leaving.*

And she believes him.

Because deep down, *she wants to be the reason a man changes.*

She wants to be the woman who was so unforgettable that he left the safety of his entire life just to be with her.

But he won't leave.

He never does.

Because the whole reason he started the affair was to *escape responsibility*, not take on more of it.

So no, the married man isn't attractive *despite* the fact that he's taken.

He's attractive **because** he's taken.

Because he represents validation, confidence, fantasy, depth, and danger—all wrapped in one *dangerously convincing lie.*

And for some women, that lie feels better than the truth.

Because in the truth, men disappoint you slowly.

In the lie?

He wrecks his whole life for you.

And for a moment—just one moment—you get to believe you're worth that kind of fire.

Proof of Value

Marriage signals that a man is capable of commitment, care, and stability.

He's Taken—Which Means Someone Already Vetted Him

There's a sick kind of brilliance to it. The moment a man puts on a wedding ring, he becomes **instantly more attractive to certain women**. Not because he's forbidden, not because he's dangerous—but because he's *pre-approved*.

You don't have to wonder if he's afraid of commitment.

You don't have to guess if he's capable of holding down a relationship.

You don't have to gamble your time figuring out whether he's the kind of guy who ghosts, forgets birthdays, or treats fidelity like a seasonal hobby.

The ring already answered those questions.

He's married. Which means **someone—somewhere—saw enough value in this man to lock him down**.

He's not a mystery. He's *certified*.

And in a world full of men who dodge responsibility like it's an STD, that ring might as well be a Rolex: a visible, socially validated symbol that says, *"This one has value."*

He's Trained, Tamed, and Tested—So You Don't Have to Do It

Think of it like this: most single men are raw materials.

You meet them halfway through their evolution. You have to mold them, teach them, polish them. It's like buying furniture that still needs to be assembled.

A married man, though? He's already been **shaped.**

By another woman. By years of emotional compromise. By long conversations, fights, apologies, and anniversaries.

He's been taught to remember dates.

He's learned to say "I'm sorry" even when he's not.

He knows when to shut up, when to charm, when to show up with flowers.

He's been *domesticated.*

And some women don't want to do the training.

They want to **reap the benefits of someone else's labor**.

If He's Married, Then He Must Have Something Worth Keeping

Here's the dirty psychological truth: marriage is social proof.

In the same way a restaurant with a long line seems more delicious, or a pair of shoes on backorder suddenly becomes must-have, **a man who's already claimed becomes instantly more desirable**.

Why?

Because it validates what women are constantly trying to measure in every man they meet:

- Can he commit?
- Can he provide?
- Is he dependable?
- Will he stick around?

The married man—on paper—answers all those questions.

He *must* be capable of commitment. He's committed.

He *must* be stable. He's providing for a wife, maybe kids.

He *must* be emotionally tolerable. Someone's waking up next to him every morning and not filing for divorce.

That's not always true, of course.

But **the ring lets women suspend disbelief.**

Because in a dating world full of flaky, aimless, emotionally stunted men, the married man looks like a unicorn—even if he's really just a horse with good PR.

Marriage as a Masculinity Resume

Let's stop pretending women aren't practical.

A lot of attraction isn't about love—it's about *assessment.*

Women are constantly scanning for signs of long-term potential, even when they swear they're just "having fun."

And what is marriage if not **a ready-made resume**?

- "Look, someone trusts me with their future."
- "Look, I've passed the basic tests of adulthood."
- "Look, I haven't self-destructed (publicly) yet."

For the woman observing from the outside, he becomes a *safe investment.*

Even if she doesn't want to marry him herself, his marriage tells her:

"This man is capable of performing the duties of love."

And in today's emotionally bankrupt dating scene, that's a turn-on.

He's Not Just Safe—He's Symbolically Powerful

A married man doesn't just represent value—he represents **power.**

He has a family.

He makes decisions.

He navigates the adult world with *authority.*

Even if he's struggling inside, on the outside, he looks like he's *made it.*

And for some women, that power isn't a deterrent—it's magnetic.

Because power means stability.

And stability means safety.

And even women who've been burned before still crave the illusion that *somewhere out there is a man who won't disappear at the first sign of inconvenience.*

And if he's married?

That means he's already proven he can **stay**—even if he's lying about where he's staying tonight.

The Ring Is a Filter That Singles Don't Have

Let's face it: the dating pool is full of question marks.

- Is he looking for something serious?
- Does he even like women?
- Is he emotionally literate or just saying what he thinks I want to hear?
- Can he hold a job, an erection, a meaningful conversation?

With married men, there's less guesswork.

You already know:

- He's capable of emotional intimacy—at least *some* form of it.
- He can commit—even if he's betraying that commitment now.
- He's not afraid of a label—he already has one.

It's a **shortcut**.

A psychological cheat code.

Instead of building a man from the ground up, you pick one that's already been assembled and painted with the varnish of domestic life.

Sure, it's someone else's furniture.

But at least it's sturdy.

Even If She Doesn't Want Him, She Wants to Be Wanted by Someone Like Him

Sometimes, the attraction isn't even about *him*.

It's about what he represents.

Being wanted by a married man sends a twisted but potent message:

> "I'm desirable enough to make a committed man break the rules."
>
> "I'm powerful enough to distract a man from the life he built with someone else."
>
> "I'm the exception to a contract he promised to honor."

It's not about love.

It's about **proving she can still command attention in a world that constantly devalues female worth after a certain age, weight, or emotional experience**.

His marriage makes him a mirror.

And in that mirror, she sees **proof that she's still irresistible**.

He's a Safe Emotional Experiment

Lastly, let's talk emotional safety.

Ironically, married men can feel *less threatening* to some women.

Why? Because the emotional stakes are **limited**.

- She knows he can't give her forever.
- She knows he's unavailable.

- She knows this isn't going to become a white-picket dream.

So she lets herself be **seen**, desired, pursued—without the pressure of "where is this going?"

The affair becomes an emotional sandbox.

A place to feel again—without risking everything.

And the man's marriage becomes the **boundary that protects her from her own hopes.**

So no, she's not just drawn to him despite the ring.

She's drawn *because* of it.

Because in that tiny circle of gold lies a silent promise:

This man is capable. Chosen. Practiced. Proven.

And even if it's all a lie,

for a woman who's tired of half-grown boys and empty promises—

that lie feels better than most men's honest truth.

No Pressure, No Strings

A *married man is less likely to push for commitment—appealing to women who fear emotional dependence.*

She Doesn't Want the Relationship—She Wants the Escape Route

Some women don't need a boyfriend. They don't want the boyfriend. They're not building a Pinterest board with wedding themes and matching towels.

What they want is something *safer*. Something more *controlled.* Something that *doesn't come with expectations or obligations or the emotional trap of being someone's everything.*

Enter: the married man.

He's not texting, "Where is this going?"

He's not showing up with moving boxes.

He's not planning a future—because *he already has one.* With someone else.

And that's exactly why he's perfect.

He's emotionally **limited** by design.

So is she.

And in that mutual limitation, they find a **weird, beautiful freedom.**

He Doesn't Want to Be Her Everything—And That's the Point

There's no pressure to perform.

No need to post couple selfies.

No awkward introductions to the friend group or parents or coworkers.

He's a man with a secret life.

She becomes part of it.

And she gets all the perks—attention, passion, intimacy—**without the paperwork.**

It's like leasing a luxury car you never plan to buy.

You enjoy the ride, you feel the power, and when it's over, you walk away.

No strings.

No payments.

No obligation.

He's Not Clingy—He's Already Claimed

You know what he won't do?

- Beg for your time.
- Ask why you didn't text back.
- Push for "the next step."
- Cry about being friend-zoned.

Because he's not available to begin with.

He's already married.

He has a life, a wife, maybe kids.

And that makes him the *perfect emotional minimalist* for women who want connection **without dependence.**

She doesn't have to explain herself.

He's not going to catch feelings in a way that becomes a burden.

He knows the rules.

She knows the rules.

And for women who fear being smothered, **that's the safest intimacy there is.**

She's in Control—Because He's Not Looking for More

Some women hate the slow suffocation of traditional relationships. The slow buildup. The constant checking in. The looming question of, "What are we?"

With a married man, there's none of that.

She gets to dictate:

- When they meet
- How often they talk
- What they share

He won't ask for more, because *he can't give more.*

And she won't fall into old patterns of people-pleasing, over-accommodating, or rearranging her life for someone else's needs.

Because in this setup, **she holds the power**.

She's not the one asking to be chosen.

She's the one *being pursued.*

By a man who knows damn well he can't claim her publicly—but still chases her in private.

No Promises = No Disappointment

One of the worst parts of modern dating is the illusion.

You meet someone. You start something. You think it's real.

Then he flakes. Ghosts. Or turns out to be a grown-up child in disguise.

With a married man, there is no illusion.

She already knows:

> "This isn't going anywhere."
> And paradoxically, that makes her **feel safer**.

No future means **no heartbreak fantasy**.

No fantasy means **no betrayal** when it all implodes.

She's not being blindsided. She *expected* the fall.

And for women who've been emotionally wrecked by false hope, this clarity is **a relief**.

Emotional Autonomy in an Emotionally Rigged World

Some women have spent their whole lives **taking care of other people's feelings**.

Their family. Their exes. Their partners.

They've been the stable one. The fixer. The overfunctioner.

Now? They want to feel *without being responsible*.

They want to connect without being consumed.

They want to feel desired **without being depended on**.

The married man gives them that.

He doesn't need rescuing.

He doesn't need fixing.

He just needs **an escape**, just like she does.

And in that shared detachment, **they find a strange kind of intimacy** that doesn't require commitment to feel real.

She Doesn't Want a Fairy Tale—She Wants an Intermission

She's not looking for happily ever after.

She's not chasing the white dress or the shared mortgage.

She just wants to pause life for a moment. To feel seen, wanted, worshipped *without having to manage a future*.

The married man is the **pause button**.

She can go back to her own life when she's done.

He'll go back to his.

And no one has to talk about *next year* or *forever* or *what are we*.

She gets to be present.

Not imprisoned.

For Women Afraid of Losing Themselves, He's Already Lost Enough for Both of Them

Some women fear commitment because every relationship has meant **losing themselves**.

They've compromised. Dimmed down.

Rearranged their lives to fit into someone else's.

Every "we" meant giving up more of "me."

So now, they choose men who don't *ask* for everything.

Who don't *demand* to be the center of her world.

Who *can't* become her forever, even if he wanted to.

Because being with someone *unavailable* means she finally gets to stay **available to herself**.

So no, she's not being fooled.

She's not delusional.

She's not waiting for him to leave his wife.

She's **enjoying the freedom** that only comes from loving a man who will never ask her to stay.

Because in a world where love too often means surrender,

the married man offers something radical:

love without ownership.

desire without direction.

freedom without fear.

And for the woman who's done being anyone's emotional life raft—

that's the best deal she's ever made.

The Trophy Effect

A *taken man is seen as higher-value—"if someone else wants him, he must be worth wanting."*

He Was Chosen—Which Makes Him More Valuable Than Someone Who's Still On the Shelf

You can say you don't care what other women think.

You can say you're above that kind of social comparison.

But your brain? Your brain *cares deeply*.

Because your subconscious is constantly scanning for cues:

What's safe? What's scarce? What's desirable? What's dangerous?

And when it sees a man who's already been chosen—married, claimed, committed—it registers that man as **valuable**.

Not because he's better.

But because **someone else already thought he was good enough to keep**.

The brain is lazy like that.

It doesn't want to dig through piles of maybe-men to figure out what's real.

So it shortcuts.

If someone else *wanted him enough to marry him*, then he must be **worth the want**.

He's Not Just Taken—He's *Validated*

In the brutal marketplace of modern relationships, everyone's a product.

And marriage? Marriage is the **five-star review**.

It tells other women:

"This model passed inspection."
"This man is safe to love."
"He comes with testimonials."

Never mind if the testimonials are written in tears.

Never mind if the marriage is loveless, sexless, or on the brink of collapse.

The *symbol* is what matters.

That wedding band isn't a barrier. It's a **brand**.

And women who know how the game works don't ignore the branding—they **hunt for it.**

Because why date a man who *might* be loyal, kind, reliable...

when you can find one who's already *performing* all those roles for someone else?

Scarcity Creates Value—Even in Love

Here's the harsh psychology:

The rarer something is, the more desirable it becomes.

This is true for diamonds, Birkin bags, and—yes—**men who are already "taken."**

Single men? Everywhere.

Married men? Scarce.

And *married men who want to risk it all for you*?

Well, that's the rarest of all.

It doesn't matter if he's bald, boring, or a corporate zombie—if he's married, he's perceived as more **competitive**.

Like a limited-edition release.

He must have something worth chasing—because **someone already caught him**.

And in a sick twist of attraction, **the more claimed he is, the more chaseable he becomes.**

If She Can Get Him, She Can Be Better Than the One Who Already Has Him

Let's be real.

Some women don't just want a man—they want the win.

They don't want to be loved. They want to be **chosen over someone else**.

And what better proof of value than seducing a man who has everything to lose?

If he cheats on his wife *for her*,

if he lies, sneaks, begs—

then she doesn't just win the man.

She wins **status.**

The trophy isn't the man.

The trophy is **knowing she's better than the woman he married**.

It's not romance.

It's **domination with perfume on.**

He's High-Status by Association

You know what else marriage signals?

- Maturity
- Responsibility
- Ambition
- Social competence

These might all be fake.

But the assumption is there.

A man who's married is seen as someone who can *handle* life.

Who can make decisions.

Who can be trusted (ironic, considering he's cheating).

But in the twisted logic of attraction, **he's high-value by default.**

And women—especially those used to low-effort men—see him as a **luxury item.**

He's not begging.

He's not chasing.

He's offering something that's **hard to get.**

And that? That makes him **irresistible.**

The More Off-Limits He Is, the More She Wants Him

He's not available.

He's not emotionally free.

He's not easy.

Perfect.

Because women aren't stupid.

They know what it means when a man says, "I'm married but unhappy."

They know the game.

They just don't care—because the stakes make it *feel* real.

Desire, after all, isn't about logic.

It's about context.

And if desiring a married man makes her feel powerful, wanted, *superior—*

then she's not thinking about the morality.

She's thinking about the win.

She Doesn't Want a Partner. She Wants a Prize

Let's not sugarcoat it.

Some women aren't looking for love.

They're looking for a symbol.

And if that symbol is already married to someone else, then **winning him becomes a statement**:

- "I can get what she got."
- "I'm better than she was."
- "He was hers, but he *wanted me.*"

It's not about the relationship.

It's about **what he represents.**

To take him is to **take her crown.**

Even if it's fake.

Even if it's heavy.

Even if it cuts.

Once He's Chosen, She Can Choose to Take Him Away

There's something darkly satisfying about turning the tables.

For women who've been left, ignored, or made to feel replaceable—

seducing a taken man becomes **revenge by proxy.**

She doesn't just feel beautiful.

She feels *dangerous.*

She feels like the woman **other women fear.**

And in a world where women are constantly told to compete quietly, to love modestly, to wait patiently—

taking what someone else has feels like **taking back control.**

So no, the married man isn't just desirable despite being taken.

He's desirable **because he's taken.**

Because someone else already paid full price for him.

Because someone else vouched for him.

Because **someone else's investment becomes *her* validation.**

And in a world where women are told their worth depends on being wanted,

sometimes the highest compliment is being the reason **he breaks the rules.**

Even if the trophy rusts.

Even if it was never hers to win.

Even if it costs her more than she bargained for—

at least, for one dangerous moment,

she got to be the one everyone else was watching.

Scarcity Increases Desire

L*imited access to a man increases emotional intensity and desirability.*

The Less You Can Have Him, the More You Want Him

It's not logical.

It's not healthy.

But it's *real*: the more unavailable he is, the harder it is to let him go.

That's the power of scarcity.

It's not just a supply chain problem—it's **a primal psychological trigger**. And when it comes to men, no one is more scarce than the married man.

- He's not yours.
- You don't get weekends.
- You don't get holidays.
- You don't get mornings after.

You get fragments.

Stolen hours.

Phone calls from locked bathrooms.

Whispers in the dark.

And you convince yourself that those moments are *worth more* than what someone else gets every day.

Because your brain doesn't care that he's unavailable.

It only knows one thing: **he's hard to reach—so he must be worth the effort.**

Desire Isn't About Availability—It's About Urgency

Let's break it down:

The brain releases more dopamine (the "reward" chemical) when a reward is inconsistent, unpredictable, and delayed.

- A man who's always around? Boring.
- A man who disappears, returns, vanishes again? Addictive.

This is the same mechanism that makes slot machines so dangerous.

You never know when you'll win—so every interaction *might* be the jackpot.

And with the married man, **you're gambling for affection**.

- Will he show up tonight?
- Will he text back?
- Will he cancel again?

When he does come through, it feels euphoric—not because the moment is that special, but because **you've starved for it.**

The Wait Becomes Part of the Pleasure

In a normal relationship, waiting for love feels frustrating.

In an affair, waiting becomes **foreplay**.

You wait for his calls.

You wait for his excuses.

You wait for the moment he says, "I had to see you, I couldn't stay away."

And the less you see him, the more romanticized he becomes.

His flaws blur. His mistakes fade. His absence turns into **mythology**.

Because when something is scarce, **your brain fills in the blanks with fantasy**.

You don't just want him.

You want *what you think he could be if he were fully yours.*

Spoiler: he'd probably disappoint you like every other man.

But scarcity prevents you from seeing that.

Limited Access Feels Like Elevated Value

This is economics.

Basic supply and demand.

The more inaccessible something is, the more desirable it becomes.

This is why people want VIP seats, sold-out concerts, rare watches.

It's not always about the product—it's about the *perception of exclusivity*.

And a man who's only available in tiny, desperate bursts?

He feels like **emotional luxury**.

Even if he lies.

Even if he cancels.

Even if he's feeding you the same lines he gave the last two women.

He's not available.

So he *must* be important.

His Absence Makes You Work Harder

When a man is inconsistent, you overfunction.

You do more. You give more. You chase more.

Not because you're desperate—but because your brain is trying to "earn" the next interaction.

You send the sexy photos.

You say the perfect thing.

You play it cool even though you're unraveling.

And every now and then—he rewards you.

He shows up.

He apologizes.

He says something that makes you feel like maybe, just maybe, he means it.

And that tiny reward? It **locks you in.**

Because when something is scarce, **your brain turns it into a goal.**

Not a person.

Not a choice.

A *prize.*

His Scarcity Becomes a Story You Tell Yourself

You're not seeing him once a week because he doesn't care.

You're seeing him once a week because *he's trapped.*

Because *he's trying.*

Because *this is hard for him too.*

You tell yourself:

- "He's doing his best."
- "If he were free, we'd be perfect."
- "This means more because we fight for it."

No, it doesn't.

You're not fighting for love.

You're fighting for **crumbs**—because you've mistaken the *absence of something* for *the value of it.*

The Affair Isn't Intense Because It's Love—It's Intense Because It's Starvation

That feeling? The obsession? The racing heart?

That's not because you've found your soulmate.

It's because you've found a man who gives you *just enough to stay* and *not enough to thrive.*

It's not love.

It's emotional malnutrition.

But because it's rare, you mistake it for magic.

If he were around every day, you'd see it.

The flakiness. The ego. The excuses.

But scarcity has done its job.

You've already bought into the illusion that **rarity equals worth.**

You're Not Addicted to Him—You're Addicted to the Chase He Created

Let's be honest.

If he were yours tomorrow, fully available, fully present—

You'd probably lose interest in a month.

Because the desire didn't come from compatibility.

It came from **scarcity**.

From what you *couldn't* have.

From the sense that if you just tried a little harder, said the right thing, stayed just a little longer—you'd finally win.

But winning what?

A man who only knows how to love when there are limits?

A man who confuses being hard to reach with being worth the wait?

No.

You're not in love.

You're in **competition with the distance.**

And the more it hurts, the more it convinces you it must be real.

So no, the affair isn't intense because you're twin flames.

It's intense because **he's not fully there**—and your brain has mistaken absence for value.

Because when something is rare, you fight for it.

Even if it's broken.

Even if it's borrowed.

Even if it was *never yours to begin with.*

Because scarcity doesn't just increase desire—

it convinces you that the emptiness is part of the experience.

Emotional Safety in Distance

Women with abandonment issues may feel safer with men who can't fully be theirs.

She Doesn't Want to Be Left Again—So She Chooses Someone Who Was Never Fully There to Begin With

It sounds backwards.

It sounds tragic.

But it makes *perfect psychological sense.*

For some women, emotional distance isn't a red flag—it's **a comfort zone.**

Because when you've been hurt, rejected, or abandoned by the people who were supposed to stay—**true emotional intimacy feels like a setup.**

So instead of chasing a man who can love her fully...

She gravitates toward a man who **can't.**

Not because she's broken.

Not because she's desperate.

But because, deep down, she's protecting herself.

You can't be abandoned by someone who was never really yours.

You can't be devastated when you never *expected* forever.

You can't fall apart if you never fully let go.

The married man?

He's emotionally limited by design.

And for some women, **that's the safest love of all.**

Distance Feels Familiar—And Familiar Feels Safe

The woman who chooses the unavailable man doesn't always want a relationship.

She wants **connection with a safety switch**.

She wants love that's close enough to feel—but far enough not to destroy her.

It's emotional intimacy **in a controlled environment**.

She doesn't have to see his bad habits.

She doesn't have to get too close.

She doesn't have to risk being truly vulnerable—because the boundaries are built in.

- He has a wife.
- He has a family.
- He has a home that's not hers.

So the emotional cage is pre-assembled.

And from inside it, **she feels just safe enough to open up... but never all the way.**

The Affair Isn't a Romance. It's a Coping Mechanism with Lingerie

Let's call it what it is.

This isn't about love.

This is about **fear management**.

It's about getting your needs met in *bite-sized doses*, so you don't risk another emotional collapse.

She gets the flirtation, the fire, the forbidden thrill—without the deep, vulnerable exposure that comes with a real relationship.

Because real relationships?

- Require trust.
- Require hope.

- Require the terrifying act of letting someone *all the way in.*

And if you've been burned before—by a father who left, a partner who cheated, a friend who disappeared—that kind of intimacy feels like **a loaded gun**.

So you opt for the illusion of closeness instead.

And the married man is *perfect for that role.*

She's Not Avoiding Love—She's Avoiding the Trauma of Rejection

Some people fear intimacy because they've never experienced it safely.

Every time they've opened up, they've been left.

Abused.

Mocked.

Forgotten.

So they adapt.

They love from a distance.

They become masters at managing emotional expectations.

And when a man says, "I'm married, but I want you"?

That's not a dealbreaker.

That's **a deal she can finally survive.**

Because she knows the script.

She knows he won't be fully present.

She knows it's temporary.

And she knows how to **prepare for the ending** before it starts.

That's not romantic.

That's **emotional strategy**.

She Doesn't Want Forever—She Wants Control Over Her Own Abandonment

In normal relationships, the biggest fear is this:

"What if I give everything... and he still leaves?"

But with the married man, the leaving is *guaranteed.*
And that weirdly makes it easier.

- She doesn't expect commitment.
- She doesn't expect consistency.
- She doesn't expect a happy ending.

So when it ends—and it always does—she doesn't crumble.

Because **she never built her identity around the illusion of permanence.**

It's like watching a movie you already know ends in heartbreak.
You still cry.
But you *survive it.*
Because the pain was *predicted.*
And that makes it feel **manageable**.

She Controls the Terms Because He Can't Demand More

When you love someone fully available, they can *ask things of you.*
Time. Emotion. Commitment. Healing. Change.
But when you're with someone married?
They're the ones with the secret.
They're the ones with the limitations.
So you stay in control.

- You decide when to reply.
- You decide when to disappear.
- You decide what version of yourself they see.

There's no "where is this going?"
Because you both already know.

And that knowledge gives her something she rarely gets in other relationships: **the power to manage her own emotional exposure.**

She's Not Weak. She's Wounded—and Careful

Let's make something clear.

These women are not foolish.

They're not naïve.

They're **wounded and intelligent survivors** of past emotional disasters.

And they've learned that the most dangerous thing a man can offer isn't sex or money.

It's *hope.*

Because hope opens the door to expectation.

And expectation opens the door to disappointment.

And disappointment opens the door to trauma.

So now, they take their intimacy in **controlled doses.**

And if it has to come from someone who can never fully be theirs—so be it.

Because at least then, **they know how to brace for the inevitable drop.**

The Married Man Is the Perfect Emotional Decoy

He lets her feel like she's in love—without ever asking her to *be loved fully*.

He keeps things messy enough to feel real—without ever being stable enough to feel threatening.

She gets the rush.

She gets the validation.

She gets the storyline.

But she never has to *face the terror of total emotional exposure.*

And for someone with abandonment scars that still bleed?

That kind of distance **feels safer than the real thing.**

So no, she's not weak for falling into this dynamic.

She's not stupid for choosing a man who was never hers.

She's choosing what her nervous system can survive.
Because love, to her, isn't a fairy tale.
It's a battlefield.
And the married man?
He's not the dream.
He's **the armor she wears to avoid another collapse.**
He can't stay.
And that's the point.
Because **when every man has left,**
sometimes the safest one
is the one who never promises to stay.

Imbalance of Power

Married men often hold more economic or emotional power—making the woman feel "chosen."

He Has the Upper Hand—and That's Exactly Why She Feels Special

This is where things get twisted.

The more power he holds—socially, emotionally, financially—the more the woman on the side feels like she's *winning*.

Because if a powerful man, a taken man, a *committed* man, still breaks the rules just to have *her*, then in her mind...

"I must be extraordinary."
"I must be irresistible."
"I must be worth the risk."

And that's what power does.

It makes being "chosen" feel like a *prize*.

Because the man doing the choosing already has everything—

A wife, a family, a reputation, money, control—

And if *she* gets his attention, his body, his secrets, his need...

Then that imbalance? That power gap?

Becomes **her entire identity**.

She Doesn't Just Want the Man—She Wants to Be the Exception

Let's be dead honest:

Some women don't fantasize about love.

They fantasize about *being chosen by someone who doesn't have to choose them.*

He's powerful. He's busy. He's taken.

He has options.

He's a walking embodiment of control.

So when he texts *her* at 1AM...

When he risks his marriage for a few hours in her bed...

When he confesses, "You're the only one I can talk to"...

It hits **like a drug**.

Because in that moment, she isn't just desirable—

She's *above every other woman in his life.*

Even the one he married.

Power + Scarcity = Psychological Addiction

This is basic behavioral psychology:

The more someone holds power over you—when combined with *limited access* and *occasional reward*—the more addictive they become.

That's the married man.

- He controls the timeline.
- He controls the availability.
- He controls the emotional pace.
- He decides when he's free, when he's affectionate, when he disappears.

And the woman on the side?

She doesn't realize she's in a loop.

- She waits.
- She hopes.

- She adjusts.

- She lowers her expectations *in exchange for moments that feel like power.*

Because when a man with authority bends his rules for you, it doesn't feel like manipulation.

It feels like *proof that you matter*.

The Wealth Factor: When Money Feels Like Love

A lot of married men aren't just emotionally powerful—they're *financially powerful* too.

And in these dynamics, love often gets confused with luxury.

- He pays for the apartment.

- He buys the iPhone.

- He sends money "just because."

- He orders room service and whispers that she deserves better.

He makes her feel **kept, prioritized, indulged**.

Not because he loves her unconditionally.

But because **he can afford to make her feel like a fantasy.**

And in a world where women are constantly taught that their value is transactional—

That *men invest in what they value*—

The money becomes a *message*:

"You are worth my resources."
"You are worth lying for."
"You are worth betraying everything I built."

It's not just seduction.

It's **economic theater.**

And when you're underpaid, underloved, and overwhelmed—being the one he spends on *feels like power*.

He Has the Power to Wreck Everything—And He Wrecks It *For Her*

The emotional narrative is brutal and beautiful in its delusion.

She knows he has a family.

She knows he has responsibilities.

She knows he has more to lose than she does.

And yet—he risks it.

He deletes messages.

He lies to his wife.

He changes routines.

He creates entire secret worlds... for *her*.

She doesn't see the betrayal.

She sees the **sacrifice**.

Not "he's a man who can't be trusted."

But *"he's a man who risks it all for me."*

That's not love.

That's *ego heroin*.

And it's hard to quit.

Power Protects Him, But It *Empowers* Her Fantasy

The man holds the real-world power.

He's married. He has legal protections. He's often older, richer, more experienced.

He can ghost her and still sleep in his own bed.

But emotionally?

He's **everything she's been told to want**.

- He's composed.
- He's confident.

- He's commanding.

And most of all—**he's selective**.

So when he selects *her*, it doesn't feel like manipulation.

It feels like *elevation*.

As if she was hand-picked out of a sea of women who *weren't enough*.

She Doesn't Want Equality—She Wants to Matter in His Kingdom

Let's face it: some women don't want to rule alongside the king.

They want to be the *secret queen*—the one he crowns in private.

The one who gets the version of him his wife never sees.

The one who makes the powerful man **lose control.**

Because when a man who commands the world drops to his knees for you in the dark?

It doesn't feel like an affair.

It feels like **a coronation**.

Even if it's built on lies.

Even if he'll never leave.

Even if she's just another in a long list of women who believed they were *the one*.

She Doesn't See the Manipulation—She Sees the Message

"You're different."

"You're not like the others."

"I can't stay away."

Every time he says those words, he reinforces the fantasy that **she's the exception**.

Not the backup plan.

Not the fallback girl.

But the *irresistible*.

And the more power he holds in his marriage, his money, his job, or his voice—

The more power she feels when **he breaks all of that just to see her.**

So no, it's not just about love.

It's not just about lust.

It's about **power**, and the illusion that *if he has more of it and still chooses you*, you must be **unforgettable**.

Even if you're hidden.

Even if he lies to you.

Even if you never get anything real from him.

Because the imbalance doesn't scare you.

It seduces you.

Because when you've spent your life being invisible to men with power—

being *seen by one* feels like the **ultimate victory.**

Even if you have to lose yourself to get it.

Cultural Cues and Imitation

Media and peer experiences normalize or glamorize relationships with married men.

You Didn't Just Fall for a Married Man—You Were *Trained* to Romanticize Him

Let's not pretend this behavior comes out of nowhere.

You weren't born with an attraction to unavailable men.

You were **conditioned**—slowly, repeatedly, insidiously—by a culture that **glorifies the forbidden**, romanticizes betrayal, and turns moral chaos into cinematic gold.

Movies. Music. Gossip. Social media.

Everywhere you look, the side chick isn't a homewrecker—she's a ***mystique.***

The other woman isn't shamed—she's *intriguing.*

And the married man? He's not a liar—he's *torn. Deep. Sexy in a suit and trapped in a loveless marriage.*

You didn't stand a chance.

Hollywood Has Been Selling This Fantasy for Decades

Let's name them:

- *The Bridges of Madison County* – Married woman falls in love with a stranger. Passion over duty. Cheating, but poetic.

- *Unfaithful* – Diane Lane has sex with a stranger on a stairwell, wrecks her marriage, and the audience is still somehow on her side.

- *Scandal* – Olivia Pope is having an affair with the literal president, and she's portrayed as empowered, desirable, iconic.

- *The Notebook* – Yes, even that. She was engaged. She cheated. We cried. We applauded. We called it destiny.

The message?

Cheating is not only forgivable—it's romantic if the passion is strong enough.

And if the man is married? Even better.

Because that makes the affair *important.*

Forbidden love = real love.

Illicit = intense.

Pain = proof.

This is not entertainment.

This is programming.

Songs Turn Adultery Into a Love Language

R&B. Pop. Hip-hop. Even country music.

They all do it.

- *"I'm in love with a man I can't have."*

- *"If loving you is wrong, I don't want to be right."*

- *"He still comes home to me, but he dreams of you."*

Lyrics like these romanticize longing, normalize betrayal, and elevate suffering to something *beautiful.*

It's not dysfunction—it's *depth.*

Not shame—it's *soul.*

You don't feel guilty.

You feel *misunderstood.*

You feel like ***the tragic heroine of your own playlist.***

And culture keeps whispering:

"If it hurts this much, it must be real."

Social Media Made Side Chicks Into Celebrities

Let's not kid ourselves.

In the influencer economy, being "the other woman" isn't a scandal—it's *a brand.*

Twitter threads, TikTok confessionals, anonymous Instagram Q&As—everyone's got a story about a married man in their DMs.

And the comments don't say "run."

They say:

- *"Sis, do what makes you happy."*
- *"It's not your fault if he's unhappy at home."*
- *"Just don't catch feelings—secure the bag."*

Cheating culture has been *rebranded.*

It's not immoral. It's *messy.*

It's not tragic. It's *entertaining.*

And suddenly, you're not hiding.

You're **trending.**

Peer Imitation Is a Drug No One Admits They're On

You think your friend's situationship with a married man is a one-time mistake.

Then you hear another story.

Then another.

- "They're in an open marriage."
- "She's never affectionate with him anyway."

- "He said he's filing for divorce."

Now it's not shocking. It's *relatable.*
And once behavior becomes **common**, it becomes **contagious.**
You tell yourself:

"I'm not the only one."
"This happens all the time."
"At least I'm not as reckless as *her.*"

But imitation works like infection.
And the symptoms?

- Compromise.
- Justification.
- Emotional acrobatics in the name of being "different."

You're not a bad person.
You're **a mirror**—reflecting the behavior around you, polished by decades of cultural reinforcement.

The Wife Becomes the Villain, the Mistress Becomes the Victim—or the Star

Let's talk narrative roles.
In stories, the wife is usually:

- Cold.
- Controlling.
- Emotionally unavailable.
- Boring.

The mistress is:

- Exciting.
- Spontaneous.
- The one who "gets" him.

So when a woman becomes "the other woman," she doesn't just fall into a situation.

She steps into a ***character arc.***

And no one ever wants to be the villain.

So she tells herself:

"She doesn't understand him."
"They're practically over anyway."
"I'm helping him feel alive."

And the affair isn't shameful anymore.

It's **heroic.**

Even Therapy Culture Is Starting to Romanticize It

"Your needs deserve to be met."

"If your relationship doesn't serve you, you're allowed to explore."

"Don't shrink yourself just to keep a promise you made years ago."

These aren't wrong.

But when applied to *cheating*, they become weapons of mass delusion.

Affairs get framed as *healing*.

The other woman becomes the *catalyst* for a man's emotional rebirth.

She's not wrecking a home.

She's helping him **find himself.**

This is self-help, hijacked by lust.

And no one's calling it what it is:

the same old story, dressed in spiritual jargon.

It's Not Just About Him. It's About What Culture Said Was Possible

You didn't fall for a married man in a vacuum.

You fell for a story that had been rehearsed for you a thousand times.

In books.

In lyrics.

On screens.

In whispers from friends.

In influencers with "situationships" and anonymous confessions.

And when it happened to *you*, it didn't feel like a scandal.

It felt like ***fate***.

Because culture didn't teach you how to build something real.

It taught you that the most intense love is the one you're *not supposed to have.*

So no, this isn't just your mess.

It's *ours*.

Collectively designed. Mass-produced. Sold as romance and swallowed like truth.

You didn't invent this script.

You just performed it—perfectly.

Because it was written for you.

And the worst part?

It still makes you feel special.

Even if it burns.

Even if it ruins lives.

Even if the credits roll and he's still in her bed.

Because culture didn't teach you to love wisely.

It taught you to love ***dramatically***.

And in that drama,

you believed him when he said

you were the most unforgettable plot twist he never saw coming.

Chapter 5: Sex, Marriage, and the Decline of Desire

Why women enjoy sex outside marriage but often feel disconnected once married

She Was a Fire Before the Ring—Now She's Just Another Chore on His To-Do List

Before the vows, before the mortgage, before the arguments over where to eat and why the laundry's still in the basket—**sex was electric.**

It was spontaneous. It was forbidden. It was fueled by curiosity, chemistry, and the thrill of being wanted.

She wore lingerie without being asked.

He touched her like he was discovering a new religion.

They had sex in cars, in bathrooms, in places they weren't supposed to.

Then came marriage.

And with it came routine. Obligation. Resentment. Sleep.

And suddenly, the woman who once moaned like a siren now fakes headaches just to avoid another performance in the dark.

What happened?

Where did the fire go?

Why is the same woman who once thrived on passion now emotionally exiled from her own bedroom?

The answer isn't about morality.

It's about **biology, psychology, and the silent death grip of routine.**

Marriage Is Supposed to Provide Safety—But Desire Doesn't Want Safety. It Wants Risk

Here's the catch nobody tells you when you say "I do":

Desire and stability are *not friends.*

Desire needs mystery.

It feeds on distance.

It loves the unknown.

And marriage? Marriage kills the mystery on sight.

- You've seen each other pee.
- You've fought over the right way to load the dishwasher.
- You've watched each other break down, shut down, check out.

There's no tension. No build-up. No longing.

There's just two exhausted people who once had sex three times a day and now debate over who has the energy to initiate.

And the worst part?

The *safety* of marriage, the thing we're told to want, becomes the *enemy of arousal.*

Because when someone is always there, when they're predictable, when they're safe...

They stop feeling *sexy.*

Sex Outside Marriage Feels Like Liberation—Because It's Not Attached to Responsibility

Now take that same woman and put her in a secret affair.

No diapers.

No emotional baggage.

No argument about who paid the electric bill.

Just a hotel room.

A few hours of illusion.

And a man who wants nothing from her but her body.

Suddenly, her libido wakes up like it's been on vacation.

She's adventurous.

She's uninhibited.

She's moaning again—and this time, it's real.

Why?

Because she's free.

Free from roles. From pressure. From being "the good wife" or "the responsible partner."

She's not performing domestic duty.

She's *performing desire.*

And in that moment, she's not anyone's mother, chef, scheduler, or therapist.

She's just ***wanted.***

Marriage Turns Sex Into a Checklist—Affairs Turn It Into Worship

In marriage, sex becomes a transaction.

- "We haven't in a while."
- "Fine, let's just do it."
- "Make it quick, I have a meeting."

There's no seduction.

No drama.

No emotional elevation.

Just *maintenance sex.*

And maintenance sex feels like brushing your teeth—important, but deeply unsexy.

But outside marriage?

The forbidden sex?

That's ***worship.***

Every touch is urgent.

Every kiss feels stolen.

Every moan feels like rebellion.

It's not just about pleasure—it's about **being craved.**

And for women who haven't felt that in years, even decades, that craving becomes intoxicating.

Desire Dies When Roles Take Over

The minute "wife" becomes the primary identity, "lover" starts to rot.

She used to be mysterious.

Now she's dependable.

She used to be pursued.

Now she's organizing the carpool.

And here's the truth:

Women don't lose their sex drive.

They lose access to the part of themselves that felt *seen* as sexual beings.

Marriage often turns women into functionaries.

Not muses.

Not temptresses.

Just administrators of the household.

So when a man outside the marriage sees her as a woman again—

Not a role, not a responsibility, but a ***desirable body with a desirable mind***—

She doesn't just say yes.

She says, "Finally."

Men Complain Women Lose Interest—But They Forgot How to Spark It

In the beginning, he courted her.

Now he expects her.

He used to dress up, plan dates, touch her like a rare sculpture.

Now he touches his phone more than her.

And then he asks why she's not "into it" anymore.

Here's the dark irony:

Many married women stop wanting sex *with their husbands*—

Not because they don't want sex...

But because they don't want to feel *invisible* while giving it.

In an affair, the sex is a return to visibility.

A reclamation of self.

A resurrection of erotic power she thought had died in the laundry room.

Marriage Demands Intimacy—But Intimacy Isn't Always Erotic

Here's a sick paradox:

You think being emotionally close will lead to more sex.

But sometimes, being too emotionally close kills the sexual tension.

She knows everything about him.

Every insecurity. Every bodily habit. Every facial twitch.

There's no mystique.

No seduction.

No edge.

She doesn't want to *talk* about the relationship.

She wants to *feel* something that reminds her she's still capable of being undone.

And if the only place she feels that is **outside** the marriage—

Then that's where her body will go.

Cheating Doesn't Always Mean She Fell Out of Love—Sometimes, It Means She Fell Out of Feeling

Most women don't cheat because they're cold.

They cheat because they're ***numb.***

Marriage made her a partner, a planner, a rock.

But it didn't make her *feel alive*.

Not anymore.

She loves him.

But she doesn't desire him.

And she doesn't desire him because **he stopped seeing her as someone to be desired**.

So she finds someone who does.

And in that moment of betrayal, **she reclaims the part of herself that marriage buried under responsibility**.

So no, it's not that women lose interest in sex.

It's that ***marriage often loses interest in seduction***.

And when sex becomes duty instead of discovery,

When intimacy becomes routine instead of romance,

When the man stops seeing the woman as a mystery and starts treating her like furniture—

She doesn't stop wanting.

She just stops *waiting*.

Because desire doesn't die.

It just goes looking for somewhere else to live.

And sometimes?

That place isn't under the same roof where she keeps the wedding photos.

Routine and the Death of Desire

Familiarity kills mystery, a key ingredient for female arousal.

He Used to Make Her Heart Race—Now He Just Snores Louder Than the Baby Monitor

Once upon a time, he was a stranger who made her nervous.

She got butterflies when his name lit up her phone.

She checked her reflection twice before every date.

Sex felt like discovery—like climbing into the unknown and setting it on fire.

Now?

Now he leaves the door open while he poops.

Now he clips his toenails during Netflix.

Now he wears the same pair of boxers until they can walk on their own.

The mystery is dead.

And with it? **Her desire.**

Because what no one tells you is this:

Routine isn't just boring—it's *desire's most efficient assassin*.

Familiarity Is Comfort's Best Friend—and Eroticism's Worst Enemy

Comfort is wonderful.

It builds homes.

It builds trust.

It builds safe havens.

But eroticism?

Eroticism doesn't want safety.

It wants risk.

It wants the unknown.

It wants to want someone who might still surprise you.

Desire thrives in distance.

Mystery.

Anticipation.

Marriage, routine, and constant exposure kill all of those things.

Because when you've seen a man pick at his toenails, cry in the dark, and eat cold rice straight from the rice cooker at 2AM—

you're not exactly dripping with arousal.

Repetition Is the Death Knell of Arousal

When something happens the same way, every day, without variation, the brain stops reacting.

That's not dysfunction. That's **neuroscience**.

The first time he undressed you?

Your body reacted like a spark plug.

The 500th time he unbuttons his shirt and says, "You wanna?" while scratching his belly?

Not so much.

Because what was once exciting becomes *expected*.

And what is expected becomes **emotionally neutral**.

And emotionally neutral sex is *a chore*.

Not a craving.

She doesn't stop wanting sex.

She just stops wanting **this** sex.

This room.

This man.

This rhythm that's become as thrilling as reheating leftovers.

Desire Needs Space to Grow—And Marriage Often Crowds It Out

In the beginning, there's space.

He doesn't know what turns her on.

She doesn't know what he'll do next.

There's guessing. Flirting. Teasing.

That space breeds fantasy.

Fantasy feeds desire.

Desire drives connection.

But once marriage happens, the space closes.

He's always there.

She's always available.

Everything is predictable.

She doesn't wonder what he's thinking—she knows.

And that *knowing*?

It suffocates longing.

Because you can't long for what you're *always next to.*

And you can't ache for a man who **feels like furniture.**

When He Becomes Part of the Furniture, She Stops Seeing Him as Fire

Let's be blunt:

The more a woman *knows* her man—his habits, his routines, his annoying little rituals—the less her body responds to him erotically.

Why?

Because the erotic thrives in tension.

It needs danger.

A little unpredictability.

A sense that the person touching you is *not entirely yours.*

But when he becomes your roommate, your chore partner, your "What's for dinner?" echo chamber—

The brain stops processing him as *lover.*

It starts processing him as *logistics.*

And it's hard to get wet for logistics.

Domesticity Devours Sexual Polarity

You can't do the dishes, coordinate bills, talk about pediatric appointments, and then flip the switch to "ravaging sex goddess" at 9:13 PM.

It doesn't work like that.

Marriage often becomes a business.

Two partners co-managing a life.

And the bedroom becomes a neutral zone—

Not a battlefield of passion, but a **sleep training bunker with backup diapers in the drawer.**

There's no edge.

No friction.

No polarity.

And without polarity, *desire flattens*.

She doesn't hate him.

She just feels... nothing.

A numbness that started small and now wraps around her like a weighted blanket she never asked for.

She Wants to Want Him—But Her Body Doesn't Lie

Here's the cruelest part.

She still loves him.

She still sees him as her partner, her friend, the father of her kids.

But when he touches her...

Nothing.

Not because she's cold.

Not because she's broken.

But because her ***body is honest*** in ways her mouth will never be.

And her body has figured it out before her brain:

> This man is no longer a mystery.
> This bedroom is no longer a place of excitement.
> This touch feels like obligation, not obsession.

Outsiders Feel Dangerous, Erotic, Unknown—Because They *Are*

Now throw in a stranger.

A colleague.

A man who flirts without permission.

Who looks at her like she's *a question he wants to solve.*

Her body reacts.

Instantly.

Not because she wants to cheat.

Not because she loves someone else.

But because ***that man is still a mystery.***

He hasn't seen her cry in sweatpants.

He hasn't watched her birth children.

He doesn't know her every insecurity.

To him, she's still *a fantasy.*

To her, *he is too.*

And for a brief moment, her body remembers what it's like to ***be a fire, not a routine.***

So no, she didn't lose desire.

Routine murdered it.

Slowly. Quietly.

One toothbrush, one grocery list, one predictable kiss at a time.

Marriage didn't kill the sex.

Familiarity did.

Because desire isn't about love.

It's about *not knowing everything.*

It's about longing, guessing, imagining.

It's about feeling like there's still more to discover in the person you undress.

And when you've seen it all?

Lived it all?

Folded his underwear for the last 600 Tuesdays?

Sometimes, you don't stop loving him.

You just stop ***feeling anything when he touches you.***

And you start missing the version of yourself who once blushed when he walked in the room.

Emotional Labor Overload

Married women often become caretakers—leaving little room for sexual energy.

She's Not Frigid—She's Fking Tired**

Let's get one thing out of the way:

When a wife says she doesn't feel like having sex, she's not rejecting her husband.

She's rejecting **yet another demand** on a day already hijacked by everyone else's needs.

Because by the time her body hits the bed, it's not just her back that's aching—

It's the ***psychological weight*** of managing the entire household like an unpaid, unthanked, invisible operations manager.

And he wonders why she's "not in the mood"?

Buddy, she hasn't *had* a mood since last Thursday.

Because it was crushed under grocery lists, emotional check-ins, mental calendars, and the 17 invisible tabs open in her head.

She's Doing Everything—Except Taking Care of Herself

Here's the everyday disaster:

She wakes up before everyone else.

She preps the kids. She tracks appointments. She remembers birthdays. She manages the family's social calendar, emotional thermostat, and dietary restrictions.

She keeps track of everyone's socks.

She notices when they're running low on toothpaste.

She absorbs her partner's silences, moods, frustrations.

She's the **household hard drive**—

Always on. Always syncing. Always expected to function without crashing.

And somehow, after all that...

She's supposed to *flip a switch at night and become a sex goddess?*

No.

She doesn't want to have sex.

She wants to be left the hell alone.

Desire Requires Space—And Her Head's Already Overcrowded

Wanting sex isn't about just hormones.

It's about having the *psychological space* to feel like a woman again—not just a mother, wife, scheduler, nurse, planner, or therapist.

But emotional labor? It eats that space alive.

Every thought she has is about someone else:

- "Did he seem off today?"
- "Did I forget to respond to the teacher's email?"
- "Did I get the right brand of cereal?"
- "Should I check on his mom?"
- "Is he okay?"
- "Are *they* okay?"

Never: *"Am I okay?"*

Never: *"What do I need?"*

Never: *"What do I desire?"*

Because the more she thinks about everyone else,

the less room there is for **her own arousal to even exist**.

She's Emotionally Bankrupt—and He's Asking for a Withdrawal

Imagine having $5 left in your emotional bank account,
and someone you love says:

"Can you give me $100 right now, please?
I haven't felt close to you lately."

That's what sex can feel like to a woman drowning in emotional labor.

It's not that she doesn't love him.
It's not that she doesn't want to connect.
It's that ***there's nothing left to give.***
She's been giving all day.
She's poured herself into everyone else.
And now the man she hoped would *relieve* some of the pressure is asking for more—without even realizing it.

She's a Caretaker by Default. A Woman by Exception.

Society wires women to become emotional caregivers.
Wife becomes nurse.
Lover becomes life manager.
Partner becomes parent *to the other partner.*
She's expected to:

- Anticipate moods
- Soothe tensions
- Plan everything
- Notice everything
- Absorb everything

And if she drops the ball?
She's "nagging" or "cold" or "moody."

But when she performs flawlessly?

No one notices.

Least of all the man in the bed asking why she hasn't initiated in weeks.

Because he doesn't see the toll.

He just sees her body.

And wonders why it doesn't light up like it used to.

Arousal Doesn't Thrive Under Pressure—It Shrivels Under Expectation

Sex is supposed to feel like freedom.

But for the emotionally overloaded woman, it becomes just another ***task to complete***.

And when your body is treated like a service station—

expected to offer emotional support, physical intimacy, and constant availability—

it stops feeling like *yours*.

It becomes a utility.

A site of labor.

So of course she says "not tonight."

Because her body isn't asking for pleasure.

It's ***screaming for rest.***

The Affair Isn't About Sex—It's About Getting to Feel Like a Woman Again

Now here's where it gets brutally honest.

When a married woman ends up in an affair,

it's not usually because she's oversexed.

It's because she's *over-functioning*—and someone finally sees her outside of her caretaker role.

The affair partner doesn't expect her to be perfect.

He doesn't ask her to solve problems.

He doesn't need her to do anything but *exist in her erotic self.*

She doesn't have to *earn* the moment.

She just gets to be ***wanted***—not for what she provides, but for who she is.

And in that small, illicit space, she rediscovers a version of herself that isn't buried under grocery lists and emotional CPR.

She finds her ***desire***

Not because he's better than her husband—

But because ***he's not asking her to fix him.***

If You Want Her to Want You—Stop Being Another Person She Has to Take Care Of

Here's the ugly truth:

A lot of husbands become **another dependent**.

They lean emotionally, but rarely reciprocate.

They expect emotional nourishment, but don't offer it.

They ask for sex, but don't create space for intimacy.

They want to feel loved...

But forget that ***desire requires relief.***

If you want your wife to want sex,
give her something she hasn't had in years:

- A break.
- Support.
- Silence.
- Help.
- Someone who sees her not just as a partner—but as a ***person who is drowning and still smiling.***

So no, she's not broken.

She's just buried.

Under mental load, invisible labor, and the weight of being *everyone's emotional anchor.*

Sex isn't gone.

It's just *trapped* underneath everything else she's expected to carry.

And if no one helps her unload it—

don't be surprised when the thing she's too tired for isn't just sex.

It's ***you.***

Resentment and Hidden Anger

Built-up emotional conflicts suppress libido.

She Doesn't Want to Sleep With Him—She Wants to *Scream* at Him

It's not a mystery.

It's not menopause.

It's not that she's "not a sexual person anymore."

It's that ***she's pissed.***

And she's been pissed for a long time.

Maybe he forgot her birthday.

Maybe he minimized her feelings during a fight three years ago and never brought it up again.

Maybe he said "I'll help out more" and then... didn't.

Or maybe it's death by a thousand little betrayals—small, quiet cuts that never healed.

And now, she's lying next to him, body cold, mind racing, ***heart clenched with unresolved rage***.

And he wants sex?

She doesn't want to open her legs.

She wants to ***shove a fork through his Xbox.***

You Can't Feel Sexy When You're Secretly Seething

Let's break down what's actually happening here.

Desire requires *openness*.

It requires trust, vulnerability, emotional oxygen.

But resentment?

Resentment is ***constriction***.

It's an emotional corset. It wraps around your chest and squeezes every drop of warmth out of you.

It says:

- "I remember what you did."
- "You still haven't apologized."
- "I can't believe you expect me to want you after *that*."

Resentment doesn't just kill romance.

It ***butchers*** it.

It turns your body into a war zone, where every touch feels invasive.

Even if he's gentle. Even if he's sweet.

Because ***anger holds grudges that your body never forgets***.

Sex Is Vulnerability—and You Can't Be Vulnerable With Someone Who's Hurt You

She used to open up.

Now she shuts down.

She used to crave his hands.

Now she tenses the moment he gets near her.

Why?

Because unresolved conflict turns touch into ***manipulation***.

Every kiss feels like he's trying to dodge accountability.

Every "I love you" sounds like gaslighting.

She can't relax.

She can't melt.

She can't ***trust*** that sex is about intimacy, because ***he hasn't earned it.***

Not emotionally.

Not lately.

Maybe not ever.

He Thinks It's About Sex—She Knows It's About Power

To him, the sexless marriage is a problem of desire.
To her, it's a **power protest**.
Because when she's angry, but has no space to express it—
When she's silenced, minimized, or told to "get over it"—
The one thing she can still control is her body.
And suddenly, *not having sex* becomes a language.
A quiet rebellion.
A subtle "f**k you" spoken in silence.
Not because she's cruel—
But because ***she's exhausted from being unheard everywhere else.***

Resentment Builds Slowly—Then Explodes in Bed

It didn't start with a fight.
It started with:

- The dishes he left "soaking."
- The nights he said, "Just five more minutes," and never came to bed.
- The times she had to explain how to load the dishwasher *again*.
- The emotional labor he didn't even notice she was carrying.

Each moment seems small.
Trivial.
Forgettable.
But resentment is a slow rot.
And it always collects interest.
Until suddenly, she can't even *look at him* without feeling bitterness in her bones.
And she can't even *imagine* having sex without wanting to scream.

He Feels Rejected—She Feels Betrayed

He says:

> "Why don't you want me anymore?"

> She thinks: "Why would I give you *that part* of me when you've done nothing to deserve it?"

Because in her mind, sex isn't just an act.

It's ***emotional access.***

And you don't give emotional access to someone who makes you feel invisible, neglected, or chronically unheard.

It's not rejection.

It's ***self-protection.***

She's not withholding intimacy.

She's ***withdrawing from a man who keeps wounding her—and expecting her to be soft anyway.***

The Bed Becomes the Battlefield

It's where he wants closeness.

And where she feels invaded.

It's where he asks for affection.

And where she silently catalogs every unresolved issue he's pretending didn't happen.

And so she turns away.

Shuts down.

And if she does say yes?

It's not passion.

It's ***compliance.***

Which is even more devastating.

Because now he's touching a woman who's there ***in body only.***

Real Desire Requires Real Resolution

You can't fix a sexless marriage with lingerie.

You can't reignite passion with flowers after a month of emotional distance.

You can't fake desire when ***what's broken is trust, not libido.***

If she's resentful, ***sex is not foreplay***.

Accountability is.

- "I'm sorry I dismissed you."
- "You were right, and I didn't want to admit it."
- "I haven't been showing up."
- "Tell me what you need from me—emotionally, not just physically."

Until those words are said and ***meant***?

Her body will not respond.

Because it knows ***this man is not emotionally safe yet.***

So no, she's not "cold."

She's ***boiling with everything she's been told to swallow***.

And no, the problem isn't her sex drive.

It's ***the resentment that built up while he kept pretending everything was fine.***

Desire doesn't die because she aged.

It dies because ***she's been emotionally bleeding in silence—and nobody bothered to bring her a bandage.***

Eroticization of Power Imbalance

Affairs can feel thrilling because of dominance or secrecy—missing in marriage.

He's In Control. She's On Edge. And That's Exactly Why It's So Hot.

Let's be honest: not all desire is soft, romantic, or equal.

Some desire is messy.

Imbalanced.

Charged.

Built on the ***thrill of power, secrecy, and submission.***

And that's exactly what marriage tends to kill.

Because marriage is supposed to be balanced.

Safe.

Mutual.

Predictable.

And while that's great for financial planning and chore charts, it's absolute ***poison for erotic tension.***

Because desire doesn't care about fairness.

It doesn't want safety.

It wants ***danger with a condom on.***

And the married man—the boss, the older guy, the secret lover—he represents ***everything that married sex forgot how to be***:

Dominant. Forbidden. Powerful. Unpredictable.

Power Isn't Just a Kink—It's a Shortcut to Emotional Electricity

A man with power walks differently.

He speaks like he knows he'll be listened to.

He doesn't ask—he *tells.*

He doesn't beg—he *decides.*

And in a world where many women are emotionally exhausted from being in control all the time,

that energy hits like ***lightning to the thighs.***

She doesn't want to dominate everything.

She wants ***relief*** from her own competence.

From managing everyone else's chaos.

From being strong all the damn time.

The married man, the older man, the man in a position of authority—

He becomes the fantasy because ***he has the audacity to take what he wants.***

Even when he shouldn't.

The Illegality *Is* the Turn-On

Let's drop the act:

The fact that he's not supposed to be doing this is half the reason it feels so intense.

- The lies.
- The sneaking.
- The late-night texts.
- The hotel rooms with fake names.
- The whispered "I shouldn't be here" before pulling her dress up anyway.

That's ***drama.***

That's ***adrenaline.***

That's ***fantasy fuel.***

And it stands in sharp contrast to married sex, which has become ***more about logistics than lust.***

In marriage, it's:

- "Did you take out the trash?"
- "Do you want to tonight?"
- "After the kids are asleep?"
- "Make it quick, I have work tomorrow."

Where's the ***edge*** in that?

Where's the ***seduction***?

The affair?

It doesn't ask for permission.

It ***acts.***

And that kind of sexual aggression—when consensual—is ***intoxicating.***

In Marriage, She's an Equal. In the Affair, She Gets to Be Powerless—and That's the Point

Now, this isn't about weakness.

It's about ***relief.***

In marriage, she's a partner.

She negotiates. Plans. Shares emotional labor. Argues about fairness.

But in the affair?

She doesn't have to ***perform competence.***

She just has to ***surrender.***

And that surrender isn't degradation—it's ***freedom.***

Freedom from always being in charge.

Freedom from being "the wife" or "the mom."

Freedom to be ***undone*** by someone who sees her not as a co-parent or roommate,

but as ***a thing he wants to devour.***

The Power Dynamic Creates Fantasy—Not Fairness

Let's be very clear:

Affairs don't feel good because they're morally right.

They feel good because they're ***psychologically rich.***

They tap into primal dynamics that modern relationships try to flatten in the name of equality.

- The older man who knows more.
- The boss who makes the rules.
- The man who chooses *her*, even though he has everything to lose.
- The one who whispers "Mine" in her ear like it's a commandment, not a suggestion.

These moments feel ***like theater.***

Dangerous. Over-the-top. Cinematic.

Because they exist outside the rules of marriage, where everyone's trying to be respectful, rational, and evenly yoked.

And while respect is great...

It rarely makes her wet.

The Affair Feels Like Submission Without Shame

In the affair, she doesn't have to apologize for wanting to be ***taken.***

She doesn't have to feel guilty for getting turned on by dominance, secrecy, risk.

Because it's already taboo.

There's no image to protect.

No identity to maintain.

She gets to be ***someone else*** for a few hours.

Not a wife. Not a feminist. Not a caretaker.

Just ***a woman who wants to be destroyed by someone who shouldn't be touching her.***

And that ***freedom to step out of who she has to be*** is its own kind of orgasm.

And In the End, Power *Is* the Aphrodisiac

It's not just that he's strong.

It's that ***he has something to lose.***

A wife. A reputation. A career.

And when he risks all of it for ***her?***

Even if it's a lie?

Even if it's momentary?

It creates a fantasy so powerful it short-circuits her morals and ***sets her body on fire.***

She doesn't care about the logic.

She cares that ***he couldn't stay away.***

That ***he broke the rules for her.***

That ***he still wants to dominate a woman, and she got chosen as the one worth breaking everything for.***

So no, the affair isn't "just sex."

It's ***a full-contact psychological experience*** built on secrecy, surrender, and a temporary escape from the emotional socialism of marriage.

Because while love may be about balance and equality,

desire has always thrived in the shadows of power.

And in those shadows,

she remembers what it feels like to be wanted so badly that someone was willing to wreck everything just to have her once.

Even if it was only for an hour.

Even if it was only a lie.

Sex as Exploration vs. Obligation

Affairs feel like freedom; marriage can feel like duty.

One is a choice. The other is a chore.

In the affair, she feels sexy.

In the marriage, she feels responsible.

In the affair, she feels desired.

In the marriage, she feels **required**.

And that, right there, is the divide that splits desire in two.

Because when sex becomes **obligation**, it stops being *pleasure* and starts being ***performance.***

A wifely duty.

A calendar slot.

A maintenance routine no more arousing than brushing teeth before bed.

It's not that she doesn't enjoy sex.

It's that ***she doesn't enjoy being expected to provide it*** on cue, without spark, without novelty, and often—without any regard for what *she* wants in return.

Affairs feel like exploration because they're driven by curiosity, not calendars

With a lover, it's fresh.

It's risky.

It's playful.

It's ***chosen.***

No kids to check on. No dishes in the sink. No mental checklist rolling through her mind while she fakes another orgasm so she can go to sleep before midnight.

Just raw attraction.

Two bodies finding each other in secret.

No rules, no routines, no five-year intimacy plan.

She can try things.

Say things.

Be *someone else.*

She's not confined by titles, roles, or the exhausting cycle of being a wife, mother, co-planner, therapist, and shoulder to cry on.

In that hidden room, that dim hotel, that backseat of the car—

she is allowed to be *only* a woman again.

But in marriage, sex starts to sound like a duty. A box to check. A guilt to relieve.

It creeps in slowly, this transformation.

At first, it's passion.

Then it's affection.

Then it's routine.

Then it's ***obligation***.

- "We haven't in a while."
- "You always say no."
- "Don't you love me anymore?"
- "It's been weeks."
- "I just need to feel close to you."

He frames it as connection.

She feels it as pressure.

And every time she gives in to make peace, to avoid a fight, to fulfill the "intimacy quota" expected in a healthy marriage—

she loses another piece of ***herself*** in the process.

Because now sex isn't hers.

It's **theirs.**

Worse—***his.***

Exploration requires freedom. Obligation requires compliance.

With the affair, she explores.

With the marriage, she complies.

And it's not that married sex can't be exploratory—it *can*—but only if both people keep treating each other like ***mysteries, not maintenance projects***.

But most husbands don't realize this.

They assume love = loyalty = access.

They mistake proximity for passion.

They stop seducing and start ***expecting***.

So she adapts.

She plays the role.

She smiles through it.

And eventually, she finds herself **naked and numb**, going through the motions like an actress in a scene she's tired of performing.

The affair reminds her what freedom feels like—even if it's borrowed.

The lover doesn't *need* her.

He *wants* her.

Big difference.

He doesn't ask out of obligation.

He *initiates* with hunger.

He doesn't sulk when she says no—because she rarely *has* to.

Because she wants to.

It's not that the affair is morally cleaner.

It's that ***emotionally, it feels freer.***

There are no expectations.

No silent contracts.

No evenings where he rolls over like a puppy waiting for his treat.

Just two people choosing ***each other*** without the weight of duty suffocating every kiss.

Marriage too often trades seduction for service

When marriage becomes a job, sex becomes a **shift**.

And what turns a woman on faster than anything else is ***not being needed—but being pursued.***

But most husbands stop pursuing.

They stop discovering.

They stop ***seducing***.

They ask for sex the same way they ask for dinner:

- "Wanna tonight?"
- "We haven't in a while."
- "I'm horny."

Where's the fire?

Where's the thrill?

Where's the ***dangerous, selfish need to explore*** her body like it's uncharted territory?

Gone.

Now it's Tuesday night, 9:45 PM, lights off, side of the bed, same three moves, finish in five, kiss on the cheek, lights out.

And she's supposed to crave that?

She doesn't need a new man—she needs a new *feeling*

The affair gives her that feeling.

That ***rising heat in her chest when someone undresses her with their eyes.***

That ***thrill of being watched, wanted, and chased.***

That ***freedom to say yes because she feels like it—not because she's supposed to.***

She rediscovers that ***sex is supposed to be an adventure, not an assignment.***

And that revelation doesn't make her cruel.

It makes her ***awake***.

So no, she didn't cheat because she lost her morals.

She cheated because ***she lost her autonomy.***

In marriage, sex became another expectation.

In the affair, it became ***a rebellion against becoming invisible.***

Because sometimes, the difference between dead bedrooms and burning ones

is simply this:

Whether she's there because she *wants* to be,

or because she feels like she *has* to be.

Hormonal Shifts and Motherhood

Biological changes post-childbirth affect libido, especially if unsupported by the partner.

She Pushed Out a Human—And He's Still Wondering Why She's Not in the Mood

She didn't just give birth to a child.

She gave birth to a **new identity**.

And with that identity came a flood of hormonal chaos, physical trauma, emotional recalibration, and *zero space to feel erotic.*

But instead of getting support, what she gets is this:

- "When can we have sex again?"
- "It's been six weeks..."
- "I miss us."

He misses ***sex***.

She misses ***herself.***

Because after the baby, her libido didn't just vanish—it got **buried under milk stains, midnight feedings, body pain, identity crisis, and a husband who's somehow still expecting her to be his sex goddess with a baby strapped to her chest.**

Her Body Became a Machine—And Nobody Asked How She Felt About It

Once a woman becomes a mother, her body stops being ***hers.***

She becomes a food source.

A mattress for skin-to-skin contact.

A 24/7 emergency responder with a baby monitor for a brain.

She is **touched all day**—but never ***desired.***

Held all night—but never ***worshipped.***

Needed constantly—but never ***nurtured in return***.

And somewhere in that hormonal haze,

desire doesn't just fade.

It *evaporates*.

Because ***no one wants to fk*** *when they feel like a function***.

Let's Talk Hormones—Because This Isn't Just Emotional, It's Chemical

Postpartum is not just a "tired phase."

It's a **full-body hormonal hurricane.**

- Estrogen plummets.
- Progesterone drops.
- Testosterone—yes, the libido hormone—tanks.
- Oxytocin floods (for the baby, not the husband).
- Prolactin rises (to support breastfeeding), which **kills sexual desire**.

Add to that **sleep deprivation**, vaginal trauma, C-section scars, leaking breasts, and internalized pressure to bounce back in six weeks?

You're not looking at a sex drive.

You're looking at ***a woman hanging on by a hormone-soaked thread***.

And yet, society—and sometimes her husband—***expect her to flip the switch back on like she's still 25, child-free, and emotionally intact.***

She Doesn't Feel Sexy—She Feels *Scrutinized*

Let's not pretend postpartum bodies are universally celebrated.
She sees it in his eyes:

- The subtle glances at the belly that hasn't "bounced back."
- The awkwardness around stretch marks or leaking milk.
- The way he touches her differently, less urgently, more tentatively—like a fragile thing, not a ***desired one***.

And she notices.
She notices ***everything.***
And that makes sex feel less like connection
and more like ***a physical exam*** she didn't consent to.

When He Doesn't Step Up, She Shuts Down

Libido isn't just hormonal.
It's *contextual.*
And nothing kills sexual desire like ***an absent partner who thinks watching the baby for ten minutes is parenting.***
She doesn't want to be touched by a man who:

- Sleeps through the baby's crying.
- Acts like loading the dishwasher is a heroic act.
- Thinks "helping" means asking, "What do you need?" while scrolling on his phone.

If she has to carry the baby, the household, her own bleeding body *and* his emotional cluelessness?
Then she's not sleeping with him.
Because ***sleeping with him would feel like betrayal—to herself.***

He Wants Her to Be Erotic—But He's Never Once Helped Her *Feel Like a Woman Again*

She wants to be sexual again.

She wants to be touched—not as a mother, but as ***a woman.***

She wants to feel seen again.

But he doesn't try.

He doesn't seduce.

He doesn't create space for her healing.

He just ***waits for her to go back to normal.***

But there is no "normal" anymore.

There's only ***a new body, a new brain, and a woman desperately trying to feel human again***.

And if he can't meet her there?

If he only sees what he's *missing*, not what she's *managing*?

Then he's not a partner.

He's a liability.

And sex with a liability?

Not happening.

Motherhood Is Transformation—But Most Men Are Still Asking for the Old Version

She's not who she was.

She can't be.

Motherhood rearranged her hormones, her priorities, her sleep, her body, and her **concept of self.**

She bled for this child.

She became a vessel.

She gave life.

And now she's being ***asked to perform like nothing changed***?

Let's be real—if *he* had stitches in his most sensitive parts, blood coming out of nowhere, and a sleep deficit that could qualify as torture, he wouldn't be asking for sex.

He'd be asking for ***a medal.***

She doesn't need a medal.

She needs ***understanding***.

She needs ***support.***

She needs ***to be held without being expected.***

Because sex won't come back just because six weeks passed.

It'll come back when ***she feels safe, seen, and sovereign over her own body again.***

Affairs Offer What Marriage Post-Motherhood Often Doesn't: Emotional Detachment and Erotic Reclamation

So what happens when she doesn't get that?

What happens when she's still drowning, and her husband keeps asking for ***the one part of her she can't give?***

She splits.

She finds desire in someone who doesn't know her as a mother.

Who doesn't need anything from her.

Who doesn't expect her to **function**—just to ***feel.***

She rediscovers that ***her body is still capable of hunger—just not with the man who forgot how to make her feel alive.***

So no, it's not that she's broken.

It's that she **rebuilt herself in the fires of childbirth**—

and the man she shares a bed with never once asked what that *felt like.*

Her libido didn't disappear.

It just got buried under ***hormones, exhaustion, and a partner who only missed her body, not her pain.***

If you want her back?

Don't ask for sex.

Ask ***what it's like to become a mother and still feel invisible.***

Then shut up. Listen.

And ***hold her like she's still a woman who deserves to be desired—because she is.***

Boredom with Predictability

Newness and novelty fuel female desire more than stability.

She Knew Exactly What He'd Do Tonight—And That's Why She Didn't Want Him

He kissed her cheek.

He brushed his teeth.

He turned off the light.

He rolled over and said, "Wanna?"

That was it.

The whole seduction.

The entire ritual.

The ***same script*** every Tuesday since the kids started school.

And she didn't say no because she didn't love him.

She said no because ***she already knew how it would end.***

There's no curiosity.

No mystery.

No ***spark***.

Just predictability—

that slow, dependable killer of erotic energy hiding in plain sight.

She Doesn't Want Chaos—She Wants the *Unexpected*

People think women want safety.

And they do.

Emotionally.

Relationally.

Financially.

But when it comes to ***desire***?

Desire doesn't crave a five-year plan.
Desire doesn't want comfort.
Desire ***thrives on uncertainty.***

- Who is he today?
- What will he do to me tonight?
- Will he touch me like he can't help himself, or will he just go to sleep again?

The problem isn't that he's predictable.
The problem is that ***he's so predictable it's like having sex with a calendar.***

Novelty Isn't Shallow—It's Neurological

Let's get scientific for a second.
The brain releases dopamine in response to *new stimuli.*
New faces.
New situations.
New sensations.
This is why affairs feel electric.
This is why the beginning of a relationship feels like being on drugs.
But in marriage?
After years of the same hands, same rhythm, same sigh at the end?
The brain stops reacting.
It doesn't say "This is boring."
It says ***"I've already catalogued this. I don't need to wake up for it anymore."***
That's not a character flaw.
That's ***biology.***
And pretending it doesn't exist doesn't make it go away.
It just makes women ***feel broken for wanting more.***

Predictability Isn't Just Boring—It's Erotic Starvation

Every time he says, "Let's do it real quick,"

Every time he kisses her the exact same way,

Every time he pulls out the ***two positions he mastered in 2009*** and thinks that's enough...

She dies a little.

Not because she needs fireworks every night.

But because ***her desire needs to be provoked, not pacified.***

She wants to wonder:

- What if he grabbed my hair?
- What if he planned something?
- What if he looked at me like he was starving, not scheduling?

But he doesn't.

He's comfortable.

He's consistent.

He's ***boring***.

And the worst part?

He doesn't even know.

Affairs Offer the Thrill of the Unscripted

The new man doesn't know her routine.

He doesn't know the right time to initiate.

He doesn't have a checklist.

He doesn't ***ask*** for sex—he ***pursues*** it.

He's ***risking something***.

And that makes it feel dangerous.

Raw.

Alive.

He texts her unexpectedly.

He whispers things her husband never dared to say.

He makes her ***blush***.
And that blush isn't just sexual.
It's ***resurrection.***
Because when you've been dead inside a bedroom for years,
even the ***possibility*** of novelty feels like a lifeline.

Routine Feels Like Security Until It Starts to Feel Like a Prison

He thinks:

> "She should feel lucky—we have stability."

She thinks:

> "I would burn this whole house down for one night where I feel like I don't know what's going to happen next."

He thinks:

> "I'm consistent."

She thinks:

> "You are ***reliable and completely unarousing***."

Because predictability may be good for building a life.
But ***no one masturbates to reliability.***

When He Stops Being a Question, She Stops Being Curious

In the beginning, she used to fantasize:

- "What will he do when he sees me?"
- "What's he like in bed?"
- "Will he be rough or soft?"

Now she knows.

Too well.

He's soft.

And fast.

And then he falls asleep with his mouth open.

There's nothing left to discover.

So ***there's nothing left to want.***

Desire Isn't Dead—It's Dormant From Repetition

She still wants to be ravished.

She still wants to scream.

She still wants to feel like ***a woman being devoured by a man who doesn't care about the laundry tomorrow.***

But routine has put her in a trance.

She's not numb.

She's ***bored.***

And boredom is the ***silent killer of erotic possibility***.

Newness Doesn't Mean New People—It Means New Energy

Before you assume she needs someone else, let's be clear:

She doesn't need ***a new man***.

She needs ***a new experience of the man she already has.***

- Change the pattern.
- Break the rhythm.
- Take initiative.
- Flirt.
- Shock her.
- Make her feel ***unprepared.***

Because what she's craving isn't chaos—it's ***uncertainty that excites her, not exhausts her.***

So no, she didn't cheat because she's a sex addict.

She didn't lose interest because she's old or hormonal or emotionally distant.

She just got ***bored with the same goddamn script.***

Desire doesn't die from age.

It dies from ***overexposure to the expected.***

And when marriage turns into a routine she can recite in her sleep—

she'll start dreaming of someone, somewhere, who might forget the steps...

and actually make her feel alive again.

Emotional Cheating and Online Affairs

W*omen may seek emotional or sexual satisfaction elsewhere due to unmet needs.*

She Didn't Go Looking for Someone—She Went Looking for Herself

It didn't start with naked pics.

It started with a comment.

A like.

A DM that said, *"You look beautiful in that photo."*

Not because it was profound.

But because ***he noticed.***

Because someone—anyone—***saw her.***

And when you've been living in a house where you feel more like a lamp than a woman, where your husband walks past you with a grunt, and intimacy is scheduled like dental cleanings—

that one message becomes ***oxygen.***

She didn't mean to cheat.

She meant to ***feel human again.***

Online Isn't Innocent—It's Just Easier to Deny

Let's drop the act.

"Emotional affairs" aren't some mild, downgraded version of infidelity.

They're ***gateway drugs to full-blown betrayal.***

But unlike physical cheating, ***you don't have to undress to cross the line***.

You just have to **start wanting someone else to see you more than your spouse does.**

And the worst part?

She'll defend it.

Because she's not in a hotel. She's not in another bed. She's ***"just talking."***

But talking becomes craving.

Craving becomes flirting.

Flirting becomes *sexting at midnight while your husband is snoring next to you.*

And suddenly, ***she's not yours anymore.***

Not emotionally.

Not mentally.

Not digitally.

It's Not About the Other Man—It's About the Mirror He Provides

The man on the other end of the phone isn't magic.

He probably has back pain and a boring job and a weird sock habit.

But she's not falling for *him*.

She's falling for ***how she feels when he speaks to her.***

Because he's not just chatting.

He's ***reflecting back a version of her she thought was gone.***

The sensual her.

The funny her.

The *wanted* her.

He doesn't see the mother, the manager, the one carrying all the emotional weight.

He sees ***a woman.***

And when you've been starving for that kind of recognition, ***you'll keep logging in like it's heroin.***

Women Don't Cheat to Escape Sex—They Cheat to Escape *Neglect*

This isn't about horniness.

It's about ***starvation.***

And when a woman is emotionally starved, ***attention becomes arousal.***

Her husband doesn't ask how she's feeling.

But this guy online checks in every day.

Her husband talks about bills and car maintenance.

This guy asks what she's wearing under her hoodie.

And the more her partner fails to notice she's drifting,

the closer she moves toward ***the man who noticed everything.***

Digital Affairs Feel Safer—But They Wound Just As Deep

There's no lipstick on the collar.

No hotel receipt.

No telltale hickeys.

But emotionally?

She's ***gone***.

Because even if her body hasn't left the marriage,

her ***heart's already moved out and is sleeping in someone else's inbox.***

And when your wife starts hiding her phone, staying up late to "scroll," smiling at messages she doesn't tell you about—

you haven't just lost her attention.

You've lost ***her intimacy.***

Online Affairs Allow Women to Control the Fantasy

Unlike real-life cheating, the internet gives her ***full creative control.***

She picks the version of herself she wants to present.

She curates her replies.

She edits her photos.

She builds ***the fantasy of who she used to be*** before life wore her down.

And because she never has to reveal the mess of her real life, she can ***stay in the fantasy longer***.

No dishes.

No deadlines.

No diapers.

Just dopamine and someone who never saw her clean a toilet with tears in her eyes.

She Feels Guilty—But Not Enough to Stop

She knows it's wrong.

She knows she's hiding.

She knows it's not sustainable.

But ***for the first time in months—maybe years—she feels alive.***

She feels desirable.

Not like a partner.

Not like a teammate.

But like ***a woman*** who still has the power to make a man lose sleep.

And if her husband finds out, he'll be outraged.

Shocked.

Devastated.

But he won't ask the real question:

> ***"What part of you did I stop seeing that made someone else so irresistible?"***

Online Affairs Don't End With Logouts—They End With Consequences

You can't "just delete the app."

Because ***the app wasn't the problem***.

The problem was:

- The years of emotional neglect.
- The passive routine.

- The dead bedroom.
- The failure to ask her ***what she needs to feel wanted again.***

And until those wounds are acknowledged,
she's going to keep going back.
To a new man.
Or a new app.
Or a new fantasy.
Because what she's addicted to isn't ***cheating***.
It's ***the feeling of being seen again***.

So no, she didn't fall for a stranger on the internet because she's reckless.

She fell because ***you stopped looking at her like she mattered.***

And no, she doesn't want to blow up her life.

She just wanted to remember ***what it felt like to be a woman worth undressing slowly***—

even if only through a screen.
Even if only for a little while.
Even if it was a lie.

Chapter 6: The Hidden Cost and Secret Freedom

Why women stay even when they know—or why they leave without regret

She Knew. She Always Knew. And She Stayed Anyway.

People love to ask: *"Why would she stay with a cheater?"*

As if the answer is supposed to be simple.

As if love is a math problem.

As if marriage is a clean, manageable equation and not a battlefield of **silent negotiations, self-deception, and psychological endurance.**

She knew.

She saw the signs.

The emotional distance. The changed passwords. The sudden gym obsession. The way he turned his phone face-down like it was radioactive.

And still—she stayed.

Not because she was weak.

But because ***walking away costs more than people understand.***

She Stays Because the Cost of Leaving Feels Higher Than the Price of Betrayal

Leaving isn't just about packing a bag.

It's about *shattering a life.*

- Who gets the kids?
- Who gets the house?
- Who gets the friends, the routines, the entire identity built over decades?

And what does she get?

Judgment.

Pity.

The title of "the woman who couldn't keep her man."

She doesn't stay because she forgives him.

She stays because ***she's done the math, and betrayal is cheaper than divorce.***

And on some days, she hates herself for it.

But on others?

She convinces herself that ***maybe survival is enough.***

She Stays Because She's Not Just a Wife—She's a Strategist

Let's stop romanticizing the act of leaving.

Sometimes, the smartest thing a woman can do is ***play the long game.***

She knows he's cheating.

So she cheats emotionally.

She withdraws.

She saves money.

She builds independence in secret.

She turns herself into ***a ghost inside her own marriage*** so that when she finally walks away—

she feels nothing.

Because staying isn't always about love.

Sometimes it's about ***timing.***

Sometimes it's about ***power.***

Sometimes it's about ***waiting until you no longer care if he lives or dies before you finally take the keys and leave.***

But Then... Sometimes She Leaves. And When She Does, She Leaves *Completely*.

No screaming.

No begging.

No throwing plates.

Just ***a sudden stillness.***

One day, she just stops replying.

Stops cooking.

Stops explaining.

Stops ***hoping***.

And he doesn't see it at first.

Because he's used to her absorbing everything.

But then he comes home and ***she's gone.***

Not just physically—mentally, emotionally, sexually.

Gone like a house fire that already burned and left nothing but ashes.

And the worst part?

She feels relief.

Not sadness. Not guilt.

Freedom.

Because regret doesn't exist when you've spent years grieving inside a living relationship.

When you've been dying while pretending to thrive.

When you've been touched by a man who made you feel like ***a utility, not a woman.***

She Leaves Without Regret Because She Already Lost Everything While She Was Still There

What people don't see is that **the mourning happens inside the marriage, not after it ends.**

She cried for him ***while lying next to him***.

She begged for connection ***before she ever packed a bag.***

She swallowed her needs, her pride, her self-respect—

all in the name of saving something that was already rotting.

By the time she actually leaves?

There's no regret.

There's only ***reclamation.***

Not of him.

Of ***herself.***

The Secret Freedom? It's What She Found in the Silence

The silence of her phone when she's no longer checking for his lies.

The silence in the house that used to echo with tension.

The silence in her own mind when she stops asking, *"What did I do wrong?"*

She starts wearing what she wants.

Starts saying what she thinks.

Starts touching herself again—not for anyone else's pleasure, but because ***she wants to feel something that belongs to her and only her.***

And maybe it's not glamorous.

Maybe she's rebuilding from scratch.

But ***freedom, even in fragments, feels better than being fully clothed in someone else's lie.***

She Stayed Because She Was Taught to Endure. She Left Because She Finally Chose Herself.

Most women are taught:

- Love means forgiveness.
- Marriage means staying no matter what.
- A good woman holds her man down—even when he's the one drowning her.

So she does.

She holds it together.

For the kids.

For the family.

For the image.

For the dream.

Until one day, she wakes up and realizes that ***she is the only one holding anything anymore.***

And she lets go.

Not because it's easy.

But because ***being alone is no longer scarier than being unseen.***

And for the First Time in Years—She Breathes Without Permission.

She doesn't have to explain where she's going.

Doesn't have to worry who's in his DMs.

Doesn't have to ***negotiate her worth*** with someone who thought fidelity was optional and her pain was background noise.

She laughs louder.

Sleeps better.

Eats alone without feeling lonely.

And ***makes love to herself*** without shame.

Because the hidden cost of staying wasn't just betrayal.

It was ***losing herself one compromise at a time.***

And the secret freedom of leaving?

It wasn't just about escape.

It was ***about returning to the woman who stopped apologizing for wanting more.***

So no, it's not that she didn't know he was cheating.

She knew.

She just didn't ***want to be the only one who had to lose everything.***

But when she finally did walk away,

she didn't run back.

She didn't flinch.

She didn't second-guess.

Because for the first time in her life,

she realized that peace is louder than passion,

and being alone with your truth is better

than sleeping next to someone who lies.

Social Stigma vs. Private Empowerment

S*ociety may judge, but many women feel liberated by secret affairs.*

She Knows What They'd Call Her—But That Doesn't Stop Her From Moaning

In public, she plays her part.

Wife. Mother. Professional. Churchgoer. PTA member.

Every smile, every "I'm fine," every carefully curated post online is **armor.**

Because she knows damn well what would happen if the truth came out.

They'd call her a slut.

A homewrecker.

Selfish.

Unfaithful.

Ungrateful.

They'd say, *"What kind of woman does that?"*

And she'd say—**the kind of woman who finally did something for herself.**

Because when society gives you only two roles—Saint or Slut—sometimes the slut is the only one who gets to breathe.

Public Condemnation, Private Resurrection

Here's the irony:

The world says cheating women are broken.

Shameless. Dirty. Reckless.

But most women who step outside their marriage don't do it because they lack morals—

They do it because ***they lack oxygen.***

They've been ***suffocating*** inside perfect appearances, good behavior, and one-sided loyalty for years.

And then one day, someone looks at her—not through her.

Not like a wife.

Not like a mother.

But like ***a woman.***

And she doesn't feel guilty.

She feels **seen**.

And that's where the empowerment begins.

Affairs Aren't About Wrecking Homes—They're About Rebuilding Selves

Forget what the movies say.

She didn't ruin a happy home.

She ***escaped a beautiful prison***.

Because while society judges the cheating wife, it never asks about:

- The dead bedroom.
- The emotional neglect.
- The years of service without reciprocity.
- The endless pressure to be perfect and grateful at the same time.

She gave everything—her body, her dreams, her time—and was still told ***she was asking for too much.***

So when someone finally offered something back,

she took it.

Not because she wanted to destroy anything.

But because ***she was tired of disappearing.***

The Judgment Is Always Louder for Women

Let's be clear:

Men cheat, and society shrugs.

He's having a "midlife crisis."

He's "a man with needs."

He's "just being a man."

But when a woman cheats?

She's ***villainized.***

Because in a culture where women are expected to be caregivers, nurturers, the moral compass of the home—

her desire is treated like ***a threat.***

She's not supposed to want more.

She's supposed to *make do.*

To suffer quietly.

To stay loyal even if it's killing her.

But here's the problem with that script:

Eventually, some women choose to ***write their own.***

The Secret Isn't Shame—It's Power

There's something wild that happens the moment she crosses that line:

She doesn't feel like she's falling.

She feels like she's ***flying.***

Because the affair isn't just sex.

It's ***a reclamation of her time, her body, her voice.***

It's ***an escape hatch*** from the roles she's been shackled to for years.

In the silence of that hotel room,

in the arms of someone who doesn't ask her to be "good"—

she gets to be real.

Raw.

Unfiltered.

Unapologetically ***herself.***

And that feeling?

It's ***addictive.***

Not because of the man.
But because of ***what he reflects back to her:***

"You are still alive. You are still worthy. You are still yours."

Liberation Doesn't Always Wear a Wedding Ring

Sometimes, the most freeing moment in a woman's life is the one that would destroy her reputation if anyone found out.

- Not the wedding.
- Not the baby.
- Not the anniversary dinner.

But ***the night she chose herself over expectations.***
The night she didn't ask permission.
The night she didn't shrink.
The night she stopped caring what other people would think—because ***they never really saw her anyway.***

She Carries the Secret Like a Blade and a Balm

Make no mistake—
She knows what she's doing.
She knows the risks.
She knows the double standard.
And she doesn't flaunt it.
She doesn't broadcast it.
She keeps it locked away like a weapon she hopes she never has to use.
But in moments when the loneliness comes back—
when the weight of being everything to everyone crushes her again—
she thinks about it.
And in that memory,

she finds power.

Not because it was perfect.

But because ***it reminded her she exists.***

The World Wants Her to Feel Ashamed. But Secretly, She Feels Alive.

She can't tell anyone.

Not her best friend.

Not her sister.

Not her therapist, unless the paperwork guarantees confidentiality.

But in private?

She smiles.

She ***remembers.***

She reclaims her reflection.

Because while society screams *"How dare you?"*

Her body whispers back:

"Finally."

So no, she's not proud in the way you think.

But she's not broken either.

She's ***rebuilt.***

And while you're out there judging her morality,

she's finally ***breathing in her skin again***—

not as a wife, or a mother, or a martyr—

but as ***a woman who dared to want more,***

and didn't ask for anyone's permission to take it.

Economic Dependence and Strategic Tolerance

Some women accept cheating for survival or comfort.

She Knows He's Cheating—She's Just Not Stupid Enough to Leave.

People love to ask, *"Why would any woman stay with a man who cheats?"*

Because those people don't pay her bills.

They don't raise her kids.

They don't walk in her shoes—shoes, by the way, he paid for.

She's not blind.

She's not naïve.

She's not spineless.

She's ***strategic***.

Because when you're trapped between betrayal and poverty, between humiliation and homelessness, you don't always choose ***self-respect***.

Sometimes you choose ***stability***.

Sometimes you choose ***the house with a roof over your head instead of a clean conscience and nowhere to sleep.***

For Some Women, the Price of Leaving Is Higher Than the Cost of Staying

Let's be brutally clear:

When a woman depends on a man economically, she doesn't get to throw ultimatums.

She ***negotiates betrayal*** like she's bargaining at a market stall.

- "He cheats, but the kids are in a good school."
- "He lies, but I don't have to work two jobs."
- "He sleeps around, but we eat well, live safe, and I can breathe."

She's not okay with it.

She just ***knows the consequences of leaving would be worse than the pain of staying.***

Because freedom isn't free.

It comes with ***rent, tuition, insurance, groceries, debt***—
and no, love won't pay for any of that.

Moral High Grounds Don't Keep the Lights On

Everyone loves to preach:

"You should never stay with a cheater."
"Have some self-respect."
"Walk away."

Sure. Easy to say from your ***financially independent pedestal.***

But what if:

- She has no savings?
- No job?
- No fallback plan?
- No family to catch her if she falls?
- No skills outside of keeping that household running like a machine?

What then?

Does she walk away into ***righteous poverty***?
Does she throw her kids into chaos for ***principle***?
Does she trade in comfort for ***pain with dignity***?
Maybe.
Some do.
But others?
They play the game.

She Doesn't Love Him—She's *Managing* Him

He thinks he's winning.
He thinks she doesn't know.
He thinks she's too weak to leave.
But here's the punchline:
She's not staying because she loves him.
She's staying because ***she's learned how to extract value from his disrespect.***

- She shops.
- She smiles in public.
- She plays dumb.
- She schedules hair appointments, nails, brunch with other "tolerant wives."

And when he cheats again?
She logs the betrayal like a tax accountant:

> "That's another deposit in the 'you'll pay for this later' account."

Because while he's screwing around,
she's building leverage.
Not emotional leverage.

Financial. Strategic. Long-term.

And if she ever leaves—she's not walking.

She's cashing out.

Infidelity Isn't Always the Breaking Point—Sometimes It's the Bargaining Chip

She might use it:

- To renegotiate the power dynamic.
- To get a bigger allowance.
- To demand space, respect, assets.
- Or just to quietly prepare for the day she finally says, *"I've had enough,"*

and ***walks away without blinking.***

She's not staying because she's loyal.

She's staying because ***it's not time yet.***

And when it is?

She's not leaving empty-handed.

She's ***leaving with interest.***

Comfort Is a Powerful Sedative—And She's Been Numb for Years

Let's talk about that too.

Sometimes, it's not just survival.

Sometimes it's ***comfort.***

And comfort is addicting.

- The house.
- The vacations.

- The illusion.
- The appearance of a life that other women envy.

She's built an entire identity around the idea that she's "the wife."

The lifestyle.

The woman who "has it all."

And to leave him would mean tearing down the ***image*** she's curated for years.

Even if she cries in the shower.

Even if she sleeps with her back to him.

Even if she hasn't felt desire in a decade.

Because sometimes, ***comfort is more powerful than self-respect.***

Especially when she's spent her entire life being told that ***a good woman sacrifices everything to keep her man and her family together.***

Some Women Don't Leave Because They've Been Trained Not To

Culture, religion, tradition—

They all teach her the same thing:

- "Men will cheat. It's natural."
- "Just don't embarrass the family."
- "At least he comes home to you."
- "You're lucky he provides."

So she internalizes the message:

"This is what you signed up for."
"Endure. Smile. Be the better woman."

And when she does endure?

She's called strong.

When she leaves?

She's called selfish.

When she speaks up?

She's called dramatic.

So she makes the most dangerous choice of all:

She stays. Quietly. Calculatingly. Permanently.

But Don't Confuse Her Silence for Acceptance—She's Always Watching

She's not a fool.

She sees everything.

She knows the names. The lies. The scent of cheap perfume on his collar.

But if she's not leaving yet, it's not because she forgives him.

It's because ***she's already moved on in her head—she's just waiting until she can afford to move on in real life.***

Her revenge isn't rage.

It's ***survival with benefits.***

It's ***tolerance laced with venom.***

It's ***keeping score behind a perfect smile.***

So no, she doesn't stay because she's weak.

She stays because ***she's doing the math.***

Because ***economic independence doesn't happen overnight.***

Because ***not all women have the luxury of leaving on principle.***

And while you're out there judging her from your comfortable distance,

she's surviving inside ***a golden cage she can't yet afford to burn.***

But when she does?

Don't say you didn't see it coming.

Because ***she's been planning her escape from the moment she realized***

that loyalty doesn't fill bank accounts—

and dignity doesn't pay for daycare.

Children and Sacrifices

Staying despite betrayal is often a decision for the family, not the heart.

She Didn't Stay Because She Loves Him—She Stayed Because She Loves Her Kids

People love to romanticize strength.

But they rarely recognize the kind of brutal, soul-splitting strength it takes for a woman to ***sleep next to the man who betrayed her—and still pack her child's lunch the next morning.***

She knows he's a liar.

She knows where he was that night he said he was "working late."

She knows what "just a friend" really means.

But when she looks at her children—

she chooses them over her rage.

Not because she's weak.

Not because she forgives him.

But because ***tearing the house apart for the truth would tear their world apart too.***

So she bites her tongue.

Wipes her tears before school drop-off.

And ***swallows the betrayal like another unpaid debt she has to carry—for their sake.***

Divorce Might Heal Her, But It Would Fracture Them

She's not stupid.

She knows the marriage is broken.

She knows trust doesn't grow back overnight—if ever.

She knows she'd probably be happier alone.

But kids don't care about adult betrayal.

They care about ***routine.***

Security.

Stability.

The sound of two parents clinking forks at dinner even if the silence is ***suffocating.***

So she makes the trade:

- Her pain for their comfort.
- Her sanity for their structure.
- Her freedom for ***a family unit that looks whole—even if it's faking it.***

She Tells Herself It's Temporary—But Every Year Feels Like Another Life Sentence

At first, she tells herself:

"Just a few more months."
"Just until they're older."
"Just until I figure things out."

But time has a cruel sense of humor.

Suddenly, a few months becomes a few years.

And "just until they're grown" becomes ***"they're leaving for college next week, and I don't even know who I am without them."***

She becomes the martyr.

The ghost in her own marriage.

The woman who ***sacrificed everything for the kids,*** and now has ***no idea what to do with herself.***

Because she stayed.

For them.

Even when it cost her *her entire self.*

She Became the Shield—So They Would Never Know the Storm

She takes the hits.

Smiles through gritted teeth.

Cleans the house. Kisses foreheads. Hosts birthday parties.

Plays nice with the man who shattered her trust.

And why?

Because ***she refuses to let his betrayal become their trauma.***

She doesn't want them bouncing between houses.

She doesn't want courtrooms and custody schedules.

She doesn't want them to see their father for who he really is—

Because ***he's still their dad.***

And she'd rather ***suffer in silence than make them question the ground they walk on.***

But Every Night, She Lies in Bed and Wonders: Was It Worth It?

When the house is quiet.

When the dishes are done.

When the kids are asleep and he's scrolling on his phone again—

She stares at the ceiling and asks the question she never dares say aloud:

> "Did I save my children... or just delay the damage?"
>
> "Did I protect their peace... or teach them that women should suffer quietly?"
>
> "Did I make the right choice... or just the safest one?"

And no one can answer her.

Because ***every mother who stays for the kids carries that question like a secret tumor.***

Invisible. Silent. Growing.

She's Not a Saint—She's a Survivor with a Smile Glued On

Don't call her noble.

Don't put her on a pedestal.

She's not some Disney version of selfless motherhood.

She's ***a woman making impossible choices in an unfair world.***

Where society tells her:

- "Kids need both parents."
- "Don't break the family."
- "Just try harder."

But ***no one's telling the man to be faithful.***

No one's demanding ***he try harder to be worthy of the woman holding the family together with duct tape and denial.***

She's Trapped in a Role She Didn't Sign Up For—But Now She Plays It Perfectly

On the outside?

They look like the perfect family.

Smiling kids. Coordinated outfits. Holiday cards.

On the inside?

She's dying.

But she plays her part.

Because ***she knows the collapse of this marriage wouldn't just take him down—it would take them all down.***

So she performs.

She cooks.

She shows up to school events.

She posts anniversary photos with captions like *"Through the ups and downs."*

And nobody sees the blood behind the smile.

Her Sacrifice Is Real—But So Is Her Bitterness

She tells herself:

"One day they'll understand."
"They'll thank me for staying."
"They'll know I did it all for them."

But what if they don't?

What if they grow up and ***repeat the same patterns***?

What if they learn to **mimic the same silence**?

What if the lesson isn't about love—but about ***endurance of pain for appearances' sake?***

And in the end, ***what did she really teach them?***

That love is compromise?

That betrayal is manageable?

That ***a woman's worth is in how much she can tolerate without screaming?***

So no, she didn't stay because she's weak.

She stayed because ***she was willing to burn herself to keep her children warm.***

And while the world claps for her sacrifice,
no one ever asks ***what she lost in the process.***

Not just her marriage.

Not just her dignity.

But ***her right to choose a life where she could actually be happy.***

Because ***the hardest part of staying for the kids isn't the lie you live with—***

it's the truth you never get to live out.

Silent Revenge: Affairs of Their Own

Some women retaliate with their own infidelities—secretly reclaiming control.

He Thought He Got Away With It—She Just Waited Her Turn.

He lied.

He cheated.

He gaslit her, minimized it, maybe even blamed her.

And when she cried, screamed, or confronted him, he rolled his eyes and said:

> "You're overreacting."
> "It didn't mean anything."
> "Let it go."

So she did.

She let it go—*publicly*.

She forgave—*outwardly*.

She smiled in front of the kids, took the family photos, reposted the vacation pics.

But what he didn't know is this:

she never forgot.

She just waited for the perfect moment.

Because some women don't leave.

They get even.

Her Revenge Isn't Loud. It's Clinical. Deliberate. Erotic. Private.

This isn't some impulsive "heat of the moment" mistake.

No.

This is **surgical vengeance.**

Because when a woman is betrayed, humiliated, and forced to play the role of loyal wife after her husband has treated monogamy like a part-time hobby—

she doesn't just cry into her pillow.

She ***calculates.***

She reclaims control ***not through confrontation—but through quiet, devastating retaliation.***

And nothing shatters a cheater's illusion of power more than ***being cheated on by the woman who never raised her voice.***

The Affair Isn't for Pleasure—It's for Power

She might enjoy the sex.

But ***the real orgasm is the power shift.***

She's no longer the victim.

She's no longer waiting for honesty or begging for affection.

She's no longer giving everything to a man who ***gave himself away for free.***

Now she has ***a secret.***

And in that secret?

She is ***untouchable.***

She walks differently.

Smiles more.

Stops asking where he's been.

Stops *needing* anything from him—because someone else already gave her what he wouldn't.

And the best part?

He doesn't know.

He has *no clue* that ***she already replaced him—in every way that matters.***

She Doesn't Want to Ruin the Marriage—She Wants to Balance the Scales

This isn't about ending the relationship.

It's about ***neutralizing the imbalance.***

Because when he cheated, ***he changed the rules.***

She's just ***playing by the new ones***.

He had his affair and came home like nothing happened.

So now?

So does she.

She doesn't confess.

She doesn't explode.

She doesn't ***give him the emotional satisfaction of knowing.***

Instead, she becomes ***what he thought he was safe from:***

a woman with her own game, her own lover, her own secrets.

She Doesn't Want Apologies—She Wants to Feel Even

He says he's sorry?

Great.

But she's still hollow.

Still disgusted.

Still ashamed of what she endured for "the sake of love."

So no—an apology won't fix that.

But ***a moan in a stranger's bed,***

a hot breath on her neck that doesn't smell like betrayal,

a new man who doesn't know her as "the wife" or "the mother," but simply as "you"—

That ***starts to stitch something together.***

It doesn't heal her.

But it ***reminds her she's still alive.***

Still wanted.

Still capable of seduction on her terms.

And in that fleeting, scandalous high, she finally feels ***free.***

He Taught Her Infidelity—She Just Took Notes

He showed her that loyalty is optional.

That marriage isn't a sacred vow—it's a ***negotiable arrangement***.

So she ***renegotiates.***

Silently.

Elegantly.

Strategically.

And if he ever finds out?

He won't get tears.

He won't get explanations.

He'll get ***a woman who reminds him:***

"You started this.

I just made sure I didn't end it crying alone in the dark."

She Doesn't Even Want Him to Hurt—She Just Wants to Know She Can Hurt Him

She doesn't cheat because she's vindictive.

She cheats because ***he taught her that being faithful doesn't guarantee respect.***

And she's not trying to destroy him.

She's just ***proving to herself*** that she could.

And ***that power?***

That knowledge?

That little smirk she hides when he talks about loyalty?

It's ***more satisfying than any affair he ever had.***

It's Not a Midlife Crisis—It's a Midlife Correction

She doesn't need validation.

She needs ***balance.***

He tipped the scale.

She just ***placed her own weight back on the other side.***

Not for love.

Not for lust.

But for ***justice.***

And maybe it's petty.

Maybe it's toxic.

Maybe it's **the only thing keeping her from burning the house down.**

But whatever it is—

It's ***hers.***

Her choice.

Her secret.

Her ***silent revenge.***

So no, she's not a villain.

She's not broken.

She's ***a woman who decided that pain without power is a prison—

and the only way out was to stop begging for respect

and start taking her own pleasure in ***equal measure.***

Because if loyalty was a joke to him,

then ***she'll be the punchline he never sees coming.***

Cultural Conditioning and Shame Cycles

M*any women internalize blame for being cheated on—keeping them silent.*

He Betrayed Her, But Somehow She's the One Who Feels Dirty

He did the lying.

He did the sneaking.

He did the gaslighting, the deleting, the secret texting, the "just a friend" dinner that wasn't just a dinner.

And yet...

She's the one in the mirror picking herself apart.

- "Maybe I gained weight."
- "Maybe I've been too busy."
- "Maybe I stopped being fun."

Because **in a world built to protect male egos, women are taught that if a man strays—**

it must be her fault.

Not his impulse.

Not his entitlement.

Not his immaturity or cowardice.

No.

Her fault.

Because ***she failed to keep him interested.***

Cultural Scripts Train Women to Self-Blame

From childhood, she's been told:

- "Keep your man happy."
- "Don't nag."
- "Don't let yourself go."
- "Men are visual—so stay sexy."
- "Don't be too much, but don't be boring."
- "If he cheats, make sure you didn't push him away."

So when he finally does cheat, she doesn't get angry.
She gets ***ashamed.***
Because ***society didn't prepare her to deal with betrayal—***
it prepared her to ***prevent it.***
And when she fails?
She internalizes the shame like ***she broke the marriage***—not him.

Her First Question Isn't "Why Did He Do This?"—It's "What Did I Do Wrong?"

It starts immediately.

- "Did I stop sleeping with him enough?"
- "Was I too emotional?"
- "Did I not appreciate him?"
- "Did I emasculate him?"
- "Did I nag?"
- "Did I make him feel small?"

- "Was I too tired?"

She rewrites the narrative ***to make his actions her responsibility.***
Because ***that's what she's been conditioned to do her entire life.***
And God Help Her If She Tells Someone
Because now ***she's under public scrutiny.***
Her friends will say:

- "Are you sure it was cheating?"
- "Men just do that sometimes."
- "Maybe you should focus on the kids."
- "Don't throw everything away over a mistake."

Her mother might say:

- "Forgive him. Fight for your marriage."
- "Don't embarrass the family."
- "Just make him his favorite meal."

And if she *does* walk away?
She's a "broken woman."
A "failed wife."
A "bitter ex."
But if she *stays*?
She's a "doormat."
A "weakling."
A "fool."
So ***she stays silent.***
Because either way—
she loses.

Shame Keeps Her Quiet Even When She Wants to Scream

She wants to tell her story.

She wants to rage.

She wants to ***expose him, destroy him, reclaim her dignity.***

But the shame stops her.

Because deep down, she fears the backlash will land not on him—but ***on her.***

They'll say:

- "How did you not see it?"
- "You must've ignored the signs."
- "Why didn't you leave sooner?"
- "Didn't you have sex often enough?"

And so, instead of screaming, ***she disappears.***

Into herself.

Into guilt.

Into the familiar loop of ***self-punishment.***

She Starts Fixing Herself Instead of Holding Him Accountable

She starts dieting.

Reading self-help books.

Buying new lingerie.

Scheduling couple's therapy.

Working harder, smiling more, ***faking it.***

Because she thinks maybe if she upgrades herself, he'll finally behave.

As if ***her worth determines his integrity.***

And let's be clear:

That is ***cultural brainwashing.***

Because if he cheated, it's ***his character***.

Not her bra size.
Not her cooking.
Not her ability to keep things exciting.
His betrayal is not her burden to carry.
But No One Ever Told Her That.
Instead, they told her to:

- Keep the family intact.
- Keep the man satisfied.
- Keep the neighbors talking ***only*** about how perfect they look.
- Keep the illusion alive.
- Keep quiet.

And that's how ***shame becomes tradition.***
A tradition passed down from mother to daughter.
Where silence is survival.
Where appearance is more important than truth.
Where ***a woman who speaks out becomes the villain of her own pain.***
Her Silence Isn't Forgiveness—It's Protection
She doesn't talk about it, not because she's over it—
but because ***she knows no one will take her side.***
So she shuts down.
She raises the kids.
She keeps the house clean.
She plays the good wife on the outside—
and ***dies quietly on the inside.***
Because ***it's easier to play the role than to face a world that would punish her for his choices.***

But One Day, She Wakes Up—and Realizes the Shame Was Never Hers to Carry

Maybe it's a book.

Maybe it's a friend.

Maybe it's just a moment of radical, unapologetic clarity.

But something snaps.

And she says:

> "I didn't fail."
>
> "I didn't push him away."
>
> "He betrayed me because ***he*** is broken—not me."
>
> "And I don't have to keep living like I deserve the consequences of ***his*** cowardice."

That's the beginning.

The day she spits the shame back out.

The day she stops hiding.

The day she ***reclaims her voice*** and starts telling the truth—even if it makes people uncomfortable.

So no, she wasn't weak.

She was ***trained*** to take the blame.

She was ***conditioned*** to protect his reputation.

She was ***shamed*** into silence by a culture that still thinks a cheating man is "normal"

and a betrayed woman is ***somehow responsible.***

But one day she tells the truth.

And she does it loudly.

Without apology.

Without guilt.

Without shame.

Because ***the shame was never hers—***
and the silence was never strength.

The Myth of the Perfect Man

Accepting a cheater may seem better than being alone in an imperfect world.

He Cheats, Lies, and Probably Has a Secret Snapchat—But At Least He Comes Home

She's not proud of it.

She doesn't brag about it.

But deep down—beneath the resentment, beneath the disappointment—she stays.

Not because she's blind.

Not because she believes he'll change.

But because ***she's done looking.***

Because ***"perfect" doesn't exist, and she's too damn tired to start over again.***

And in a world where dating apps are war zones, men act like loyalty is oppression, and "situationships" pass for real relationships—

sometimes ***keeping the cheater you know*** feels safer than ***risking the hell you don't.***

She's Been Told Her Standards Are Too High

- "All men cheat."
- "At least he provides."
- "He's not abusive."
- "He still comes home."

- "What do you expect—perfection?"

That last one? That's the dagger.

Because the moment a woman demands basic decency—fidelity, honesty, emotional availability—she's told ***she's being unrealistic.***

That men aren't wired for monogamy.

That "good men" are taken or gay or fictional.

That ***expecting a man to not lie to your face while screwing someone else is apparently asking for a unicorn in a tuxedo.***

So she adjusts.

She downsizes her standards.

She recalibrates her pain.

She tells herself:

"At least he's better than the rest."
"No one's perfect."
"This is just how men are."

She Doesn't Love the Cheater—She Just Doesn't Believe Anyone Better Exists

It's not that she's addicted to him.

It's that ***she's lost faith in the alternatives.***

Because when she looks around, she sees:

- Friends being ghosted after six-month flings.

- Men who think loyalty is optional, but submission is mandatory.

- Guys who lie for sport and call it "just keeping options open."

- Married men flooding women's DMs like ***monogamy was a suggestion, not a vow.***

So she tells herself:

"This is as good as it gets."
"At least I know his lies by now."
"At least I'm not out there starting from zero."

And ***that lie feels safer than the truth:***
that she might be alone for a very long time—maybe forever.

Loneliness Isn't Romantic—It's Terrifying

She's seen the memes about self-love.
Heard the podcasts about healing.
Watched the TikToks about "choosing peace over a man."
But ***at 3AM, when the house is quiet and the bed is empty,***
peace doesn't hold her.
Peace doesn't bring wine or rub her back or fix the sink.
And while self-love is beautiful,
it doesn't replace human touch, laughter, or someone who makes her feel like she matters—even if they're a lying bastard half the time.
So she takes the compromise.
Because ***a warm body, even a cheating one, feels better than sleeping alone with perfect values and cold feet.***

She Keeps Hoping He'll Be the Man She Imagined—Not the One He Keeps Proving He Is

She remembers the early days.
The charm.
The attention.
The way he used to ***look at her like she was a mystery worth solving.***
And now?
He barely looks up from his phone.
But in her head, ***she's still clinging to the version of him that felt real—***
even if it only lasted for six months back in 2014.

Because letting go of him means letting go of ***the dream she built around him.***

And dreams are hard to bury.

Harder than cheaters.

So she keeps ***waiting for him to return to the fantasy version***.

She keeps giving him chances, grace, second chances, forgiveness coupons with no expiration date.

Because ***if she lets go now, it means he was never real.***

And that truth hurts worse than betrayal.

Society Doesn't Sell Women Real Men—It Sells Them Projects

She was raised on potential.

- "He'll grow out of it."
- "He just needs a strong woman."
- "You can't give up too fast."
- "Behind every great man is a woman who stuck through the hard parts."

Translation: ***Be his emotional rehab center until he figures out how to be loyal.***

So she doesn't leave.

Not because she can't.

But because ***she still thinks maybe—just maybe—he'll become the man she hoped for.***

And ***hope is the cruelest drug of all.***

She's Not Settling—She's Surviving

She knows he's not perfect.

She knows this isn't healthy.

But ***she also knows she doesn't want to start over, explain herself to a stranger, swipe through 500 frogs, and teach someone all over again what her favorite meal is.***

She's tired.

She's scared.

And ***she's not in love with him—she's in love with the idea of not being alone.***

Because ***in a culture that glorifies couples and pathologizes single women,***

being alone feels like failure—no matter how strong or self-aware she is.

So she stays.

Not for love.

Not for peace.

But for ***the illusion that staying gives her control over the loneliness.***

So no, she doesn't believe he's perfect.

She just believes ***perfect doesn't exist.***

And in a world where even "good men" cheat and blame porn, trauma, or testosterone—

she's chosen to settle for the devil she knows

rather than wander through a dating hell she already escaped once.

Because sometimes, ***accepting a cheater isn't about weakness—***

it's about refusing to chase fantasies

when all the real men have already stopped pretending to be better.

Rewriting the Rules

Some modern women redefine fidelity on their own terms—choosing what works over what's expected.

She's Done Playing the Monogamy Olympics—She's Making Her Own Scorecard Now

Once upon a time, fidelity was simple.

One man. One woman. One house.

Till death—or boredom, or betrayal—do them part.

But that fairytale?

She's over it.

Because what society calls *loyalty*, she's learned to recognize as ***self-erasure with a pretty dress on***.

She's been the "good woman."

The faithful wife.

The ride-or-die who rode straight into resentment and barely made it out.

Now?

She's not asking for permission.

She's ***rewriting the whole damn script.***

Monogamy Was a Promise—Not a Prison Sentence

She used to believe that loyalty meant exclusivity.

That love meant ***owning*** each other's time, body, and future.

But then she watched her "faithful" husband flirt with waitresses.

DM strangers.

Treat her body like ***a relic he no longer visited but refused to donate.***

And she thought:

"If this is what fidelity looks like, I want a refund."

Because ***what's the point of being sexually faithful to a man who is emotionally absent, dismissively loyal, or just... lazy?***

That's not devotion.

That's ***performance.***

And she's not performing anymore.

Some Women Don't Want Affairs—They Want *Options*

She's not cheating.

She's ***choosing.***

Choosing freedom.

Choosing transparency.

Choosing ***the version of commitment that doesn't suffocate her.***

Maybe that looks like:

- Ethical non-monogamy.
- Don't-ask-don't-tell.
- Polyamory with boundaries.
- Separate bedrooms and separate lovers.
- One foot in the marriage and one in her autonomy.

To outsiders, it's scandalous.

To her?

It's ***sanity.***

Because ***she's done confusing exclusivity with intimacy.***

They're not the same.

Traditional Fidelity Rewards Control—She's Interested in Connection

She's not looking to own anyone.
And she's no longer interested in being owned.
Because the old rules—
"Don't look, don't touch, don't feel"—
sound less like love and more like ***a hostage situation.***
Instead, she's asking:

- Are we honest with each other?

- Are we growing together?

- Do we support each other's needs, even if they're unconventional?

- Are we ***real***, or just ***socially acceptable***?

Because ***she'd rather have a complicated truth than a simple lie.***

She's Not Justifying Cheating—She's Redefining What Cheating Even Means

He thinks cheating means touching someone else.

She thinks cheating means ***abandoning her emotionally while pretending to be present.***

He thinks loyalty is about ***not having sex*** with another person.

She thinks loyalty is ***being emotionally available, curious, and showing the hell up.***

He thinks because he never physically cheated, ***he's the better person.***

She knows better.

Because ***a man who hasn't cheated but hasn't touched her in months, who forgets her birthday but remembers his poker night, who sleeps beside her but hasn't made her come in years—***

is just a faithful ghost.

And she doesn't want ghosts anymore.

She wants ***life.***

Even if it breaks the rules.

Rewriting Fidelity Isn't Just About Sex—It's About Power, Choice, and Truth

The old fidelity contract came with expectations:

- Be everything to him.
- Don't look elsewhere.
- Swallow unmet needs like vitamins.
- Smile.
- Sacrifice.
- Serve.
- Be satisfied with the crumbs of his attention.

She's rewriting that.

Now it says:

- I will not disappear to keep you secure.
- I will not confuse silence with peace.
- I will not sleep in a bed that feels like a contract, not a connection.
- I will define what love looks like ***with you***, not ***for you.***

And if he can't handle that?

There's the door.

Because ***she'd rather share her body with someone she desires***

than share her whole life with someone who only half-shows up.

She's Not Lost—She's Liberated

The world will call her many things:

- "Selfish."
- "Loose."
- "Confused."
- "Rebellious."

But she's not confused.
She's ***clearer than ever.***
She knows:

- Monogamy isn't for everyone.
- Some marriages survive open doors.
- Some partnerships get stronger when rules get rewritten together.
- And ***a woman's fidelity to herself should never come last.***

She's not glorifying affairs.
She's not advocating for chaos.
She's ***dismantling a system*** that told her being faithful meant being ***smaller***.
And now?
She's ***done shrinking.***

So no, she's not immoral.
She's ***real.***
Real enough to admit that "forever" only works if it grows.

Real enough to tell the truth when she's no longer satisfied.
Real enough to say:

> "I will not die inside a marriage just so people can call me loyal."

Because ***if the rules were written without her voice, she's under no obligation to keep them.***
She'll write her own.
And they'll be ***messy, honest, liberating, and hers.***
Just like she is.